THE
WARRIOR WOMEN
PROJECT

First hardcover edition May 2021

Cover and book design by Ochi Ogbuaku Jnr
Email: ochi@ogbuakujnr.com
IG: ochibydesign
www.ogbuakujnr.com

ISBN 978-1-9552-3202-9 (hardcover)

www.thewarriorwomenproject.com

THE
WARRIOR WOMEN
PROJECT

A Sisterhood of Immigrant Women

Created and Edited by

Uchenna Lizmay Umeh, MD, MBA, ICF aka Dr. Lulu

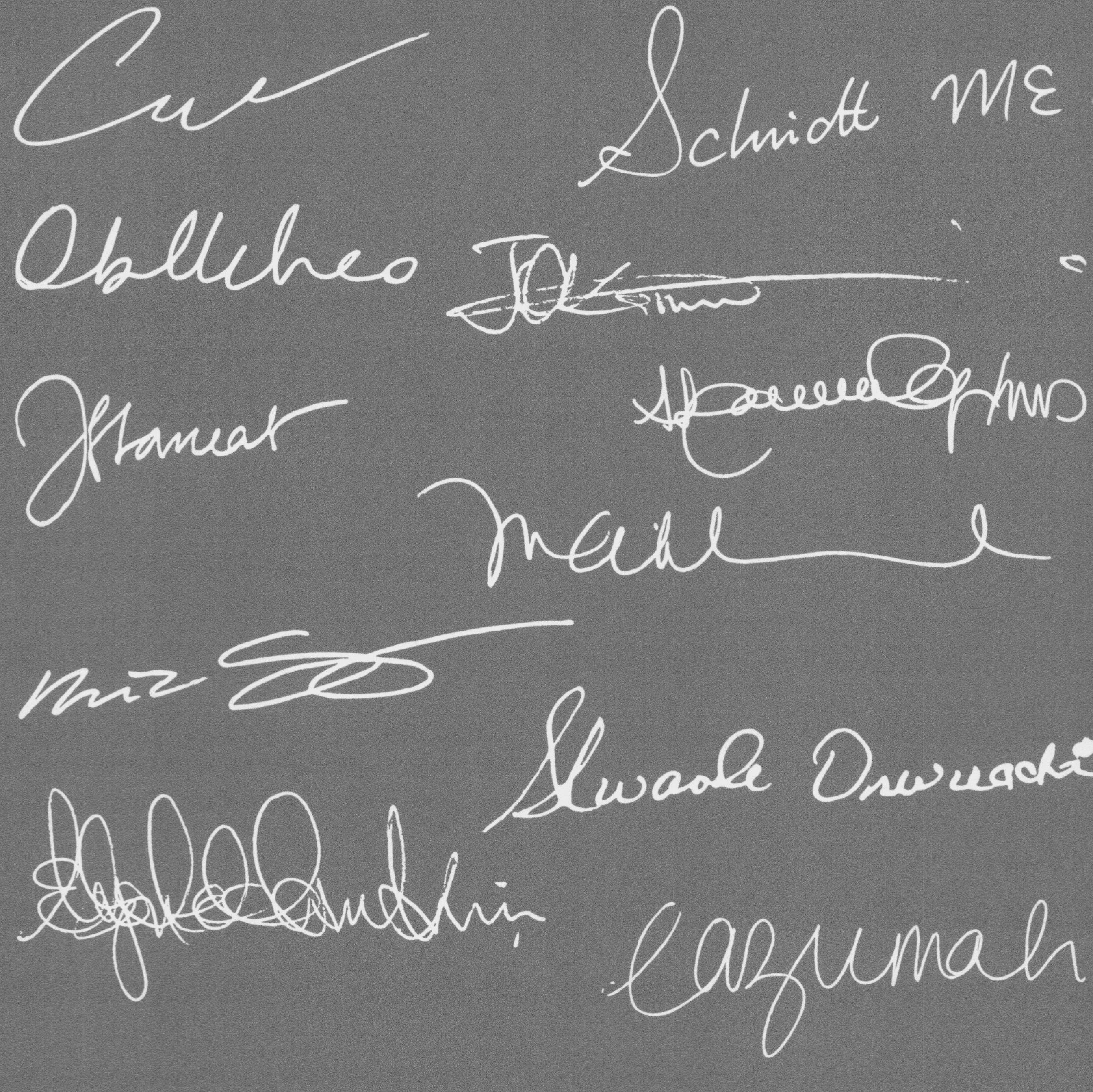
Schmidt ME.

Dr. Lulu

Pallavi Gowda

ciitoochiobi

PatBackley

Patriaceliidlen

SharonShirafn

DrKangong

CONTENTS

ACKNOWLEDGMENTS

I'd like to thank the 21 women of *#thewarriorwomenproject*. Without your bravery, and vulnerability, this book would not happen. You believed in me, and believed in yourselves, and made my dream of an anthology come true!

Honorable Abike Dabiri-Erewa and the staff of Nigerians in Diaspora Commission, NIDCOM, thank you for your unwavering support of this little girl who dared to dream.

To my website designer (*@juneplum.ca*), photographer (*@trinitygreer*), and book designer (*@ogbuakujnr.com*), thanks for sticking with me. We did it! You have helped create a masterpiece.

To my mom, Lolo Ngozi Umenwaliri. What can I say? I called and you immediately said "YES!" as my proofreader. My forever cheerleader. May your days be long, and your children continue to call you blessed. Norrin do you sis... *Udo ga'a diri gi.*

To my sister, *@shakara_com*. My most able PM! This has indeed been a labor of love. Thanks for pushing me the times I nearly gave up. You are a true blessing. May doors continue to open wide for you.

To *mis trés hijos!* My reasons for being. You blessed my womb, my breasts, and my heart. You are a daily inspiration. You will do great things long after I am gone, because you hold a piece of me in you.

Finally, to you readers, may this book open your eyes and hearts in places. May it shine a light on your path as you read it and share it.

Follow us on Facebook @ *The Warrior Women Project.*

Peace still.

Dr. Lulu

The first time I received the request from Dr. Lulu, the creator of this highly passionate compilation of stories of immigrant women, to write the foreword, I didn't hesitate to do so. Not only is she an accomplished writer (three-time bestselling author), a most commendable feat she achieved solely through perseverance and passion, she is also a Nigerian in the diaspora, and has made an impact with her work in the youth suicide prevention arena, and as a physician.

I knew I was in for a good read because Dr. Lulu's dedication and passion to change lives, empower both her peers, her clients and patients shines through in all her endeavors. She is known to produce exceptional work and it is not an overstatement to say she has the Midas touch.

At first glance, the book title; *"The Warrior Women Project"* sounds like a collection of feminist assertions, right? Wrong! This book opened my eyes to a different world of immigrant women and how they experience life, through their own eyes and in their own words.

It will take you through a journey of hope, excitement, fears, failures, abuse, uncertainties, sacrifices, encouragement, love, hints of racism, sexism and eventual stepping out into victory. These outstanding co-authors took the plunge, with unembellished truth, to bare it all in these pages, so the world can appreciate their unsung journeys.

This book is a revelation of the mix of culture, necessity and responsibility, and how they colour decisions. It thrusts self-reflection and realization of immense intrinsic potentials in full view.

The following are a few quotes I gleaned from some of its authors:

"Don't find a path and follow it, find a patch of land, create your own path, and leave a trail."

"When so many women and immigrants are invisible to the world, I want to shout out loud of our presence and power!"

"To leave a legacy for my children."

As an empowered feminist, and in my position as the Chairman/CEO of Nigerians in Diaspora Commission, NIDCOM, I see on a nearly daily basis, the plight of immigrant-Nigerians in the diaspora, so, I know first-hand what immigration can do to one's mental, physical and spiritual health.

I therefore applaud these women who have risen like Phoenixes above their own ashes to become conquerors in their own rights.

It has been my pleasure participating in this book.

A highly recommended read.

A powerful legacy that the co-authors have exemplified for their readers.

Honorable Abike Dabiri-Erewa
Chairman/CEO Nigerians in Diaspora Commission, NIDCOM
Abuja, Nigeria

"To all the little girls out there
who dream about life in a new country, we say,
DREAM BIGGER!"

~ *Warrior Women*

Time, Grace and Space

Andrea Judit Staneata

ROM / USA

My Safe Place

I grew up in communist Romania under humble circumstances in a small village in Transylvania. As far back as I can remember I wanted to make a difference, help people, and travel to see the world. I was fascinated with traveling and I would spend hours browsing the atlas and learning about far away countries and places. My favorite one was a travel atlas about Australia and New Zealand because it had the most beautiful pictures. I hope one day I will be able to visit those magnificent places.

At home, though, I did not feel safe, I lived in fear every day.

There was constant physical and emotional abuse from my stepfather towards my mom and I. He made it very clear that he hated me, and I had no right to stand in front of him. My younger sister was the favorite child, and I always tried to retreat to a corner. I wanted badly to go unnoticed as much as possible by getting lost in books and reading for hours. At school I strived to be the best student, and I hoped that one day, I would be seen, accepted and deemed worthy by my parents.

My safe places were at my grandmothers', both of them always encouraged me, told me to believe in my dreams and believe that I will do great things in life. I will forever cherish the years I had with them, and I am thankful for everything I've learned from their lifelong wisdom and experiences.

They taught me to pray and to always be helpful to anyone in need. Little did I know, that my childhood experiences would influence the choices I would make later on in life.

Fast forward, during my high school years I decided to attend medical school. My desire to leave my country, and emigrate to a better place where my future children would have a better life, never left me. That dream was placed on hold after I met my future husband just after I graduated high school. Again, I wanted to be liked and accepted, and made every effort to please him and make things work out.

There were huge red flags even prior to us getting married but at that time, I didn't think that things would get worse. I felt like I was walking on thin ice day-in and day-out. I didn't realize the amount of stress I was under all those years. I just knew it did not feel right and I could not understand why he wasn't happy with anything I did, why I didn't seem to be enough, why I didn't seem to matter as a person.

With time, things did get worse.

At one point, a therapist I was seeing, told me that I basically married my stepfather. I was confused and didn't understand the concept at first, but she explained that-that type of behavior was familiar to me. And further told me why I had a hard time breaking away from my toxic relationship.

Old Life in the New World

Winning the diversity visa lottery and basically the right to emigrate to the United States of America was a blessing from heaven! My then - husband did not want to leave, however. I did not want to give up on my dream for a better future for my family. I was pregnant with our first child and I told him I would leave with or without him. I believe my stance made him rethink, and he grudgingly agreed to leave as well. I first set foot on United States soil at 8 months pregnant.

Talk about a cultural shock! Coming from a small town in Transylvania to New York City. Thankfully we were able to connect with fellow Romanians who were very helpful during our first year. They helped us tremendously while we learned to somewhat navigate the system. I made lasting friendships and developed close family relationships which I will forever cherish.

My hope was that once we start a new life here, he would change and our marital problems would resolve as well. Little did I know back then, that it would backfire, and "everything" would become my fault! Any time things weren't going smoothly in our day to day lives, he would blame me, claiming that I was the one who wanted to emigrate and had no right to say anything. After going through the proper certification process, I was able to enter the medical training system here in the US, and on the surface we were another success story, living the American dream.

This couldn't be further from the truth, the control, and the physical and emotional abuse got worse

and we grew further and further apart. I remember during my second year of residency training, I was working endless hours and raising my infant daughter and my then 4 year old son, technically by myself. With his job in the US Army and geographical separation during the week, I was often left feeling empty,

---

Talk about a cultural shock! Coming from a small town in Transylvania to New York City.

---

burnt out and without a sense of direction in life.

I had no family support, no friends close by, and when he was home on the weekends it was hell on earth. This whirlwind of life pushed me further down into a dark place. I didn't know who I was anymore, what I liked and what my goal in life was. I felt empty! But I knew I had to push through because my children needed me.

...This Too Shall Pass

I graduated medical training and kept telling myself that things would get better once I got a real job, and he would see my worth and things would change. Things only got worse!

I felt like I was a failure and I just wanted to be done with everything and die.

The years passed and the abuse began affecting my children, particularly my son. He is older, and his father was "teaching" him how to become a "real" man. My son was having such a hard time that he begged me to leave his father and our home because he couldn't take it anymore. I was at my wit's end! My son's words were like a knife in my heart! I remembered growing up, asking my mom the same thing but

...I packed up my children, left and moved into an apartment.

she never left my stepfather. I could never understand why she didn't remove us from that unhealthy environment and I always resented that.

I blocked out those years of my life as much as I could and never thought of them until I saw myself in my son's eyes and in his desperate pleas. With the little self-esteem, mental and emotional strength I had left, I packed up my children, left and moved into an apartment. The following few years were a blur of stress, anxiety, depression and healing. I blamed and questioned myself for the longest time for everything

that happened, and felt I was a total failure for not trying harder to make the marriage work.

I had to remind myself that it takes two people for any relationship to work.

Sometimes, I wondered why it took me so long to leave that toxic relationship, and for a long time I was angry at myself for wasting all those years of my life but I have had to come to terms with it and accept it. Other times, the only thought that kept me going was a Bible verse I read right before we left Romania that I have kept close to my heart: *"For I know the plans I have for you, declares the Lord, plans to prosper you and not to harm you, plans to give you hope and a future"* – Jeremiah 29:11 (NIV).

From Fear to Courage

Today, I am at a wayyyy better place! I am at peace, and strive to grow as a person and a professional every day. My children are flourishing and I can offer them a home centered in love, respect and kindness.

I hope my story will inspire other women in similar situations.

I wanted my pain and sufferings to be gone at once and forever, like when you turn on the light switch, there's instant light and the darkness is all gone. However that is not how life works. I always try to

remember to live by the following statement - Never ever give up on yourself and on your dreams, even in the darkest moments, there is always something to be grateful for.

I did not realize what a heavy load I was carrying around from my childhood and as I was going through life, more load was added on by others or by life's circumstances. I did not know how to unpack and let go, I just knew it was wearing me down. I had a hard time coming to terms and processing some aspects of the abuse from my childhood and later on from my relationship. I could not understand why an adult would treat a child like that, a child who did not ask for anything but love and acceptance, and who could not defend herself in any way.

I also had a hard time processing and letting go of the fact that, the same person who would tell you one minute that they loved you or cared about you, the next minute would fly into a rage and call you names and hit you because something didn't sit right with them.

I experienced pain, I felt all the feelings and emotions throughout the process of healing, making peace and letting go of the past. Now, looking back, I feel like I went through a crucible which molded me into the person I am today. I believe things happen for a reason and God has a plan for me in every aspect of

my life. I also believe that there is more to life and I strive daily to become a better human being and leave a positive imprint.

The most important lessons I learned during my healing process are to allow myself time, grace and space. I needed the time to heal and to come to terms with the past, I needed grace to forgive myself and not to blame myself for everything, and I needed space to start filling it with positive thoughts and things that gave me hope.

What is your personal or professional motto?
"You can't go back and change the beginning, but you can start where you are and change the ending."
– C. S. Lewis

What legacy would you like to leave behind?
The legacies I would like to leave behind are the same ones I teach my children: always be kind, stay humble, work hard and never give up. In any circumstance, even during the darkest times, there are things to be grateful and thankful for.

If you could have lunch with one woman, who would it be?
Actually it would be two - my grandmothers. They lived and survived World War II and I would ask them about their experiences, lessons learned, their faith and what was one thing that kept them going during those times.

What is your favorite food from your home country?
Too many to list but the one I love the most is the sweet holiday bread with walnuts or poppy seeds. It reminds me of Christmas and brings me back to my childhood.

What two quotes inspire you?
"Strong people don't put others down. They lift them up."
– Anonymous

"Sometimes our lives have to be completely shaken up, changed, and rearranged to relocate us to the place we were meant to be."
– Anonymous

Short Bio
Andrea Judit Staneata, MD is board certified physician in Physical Medicine and Rehabilitation. She lives and works in North Carolina. She is passionate about educating her patients regarding their conditions and treatments available for them. She enjoys spending time with her children, reading, and traveling.

I Am a Victoria Gal!

Anne E. Burnley

CMR / USA

Coming to America, Literally!

Two days and three plane rides after saying goodbye to my parents at the airport, we finally landed at the John Fitzgerald Kennedy International Airport in New York. My gateway into America bears the name of my favorite American president and I take it as a good omen. I wait for my friend Blanche and we clear immigration and customs together. After a brief hug, we rush off to catch our connecting flights, she to Minnesota and I to Washington, DC.

I push my luggage cart into the arrival area at the Ronald Reagan Washington National Airport in DC, scanning the crowd of eager friends and family, looking for my uncle. I do not see him! I rummage through my hand luggage, looking for my lifeline. I cannot find the piece of paper with its jagged-edge, evidence it was once part of an A7 "carnet". It had hand-scribbled names and phone numbers of my emergency contacts. I cannot find it anywhere!

My baseline anxiety and an imagination unencumbered by unfamiliar surroundings takes flight. I imagine disappearing without a trace after asking a stranger for help, my American dream, aborted before its birth. My musings abruptly end when I notice Uncle Jacob. He is walking in my general direction and I take off run-walking towards him. His long, easy stride matches his stature and bearing. Uncle sees me and greets me with a warm smile and a bear hug.

Uncle Jacob walks over to the 'abandoned' cart holding my precariously stacked belongings. He picks up my suitcases like they are filled with feathers instead of clothes, neatly folded inside, arranged side by side with Cameroonian delicacies and spices. I come bearing gifts. Less than twenty minutes later, he loads me and my belongings into his car and we are on the road to his home in suburban Maryland, where my Aunty Elise and six cousins await me.

That was more than thirty-six years ago and one constant during the intervening years has been the relentless march of time.

Victoria!

I was raised in Victoria, now called Limbe, a seaside town in Cameroon, which has been the hometown of several generations of my family.

Growing up, women formed the informal neighborhood watch. They monitored us relentlessly and relayed details of our whereabouts, activities, and companions back to our parents. Cell phones had not been invented, fixed telephones were rare and reserved to receive overseas calls but word of mouth traveled at supersonic speeds.

Growing up with five siblings and extended family members in a loving but strict home, I have mostly happy memories. I say "mostly" because I also remember worrying about falling victim to grown men who preyed on children. These monsters, often cooks, cleaners and drivers, entered our house on legitimate business. My parents were oblivious to the dangers lurking in their home.

Waste Not The Mind

My earliest childhood memory was of my first day in nursery school. I was wearing a yellow blouse and a pair of blue shorts on the day mummy took me there. I was more worried about the tear in my shorts than about being left there. Education was vital in our home, coming a close second only after God. My parents were university graduates, and constantly touted the benefits of a good education.

Growing up, women formed the informal neighborhood watch.

Mummy often told me that it was better to give my best effort and fail a class, than to get a mediocre grade because I did not apply myself. The seemingly benign comment "Could do better" on my report card and favored by teachers all around the world, was a harbinger of many scoldings. Mummy took this to mean I was not living up to my full God-given potential, in other words, I was "wasting my mind."

South By Southwest

One week after arriving in Maryland, I boarded another plane for Austin, Texas, to begin my first year

at St. Edward's University. Back then Austin was best known as the capital of Texas and a university town. There were no music festivals that I remember and I knew nothing about technology outside of microfiche and microfilm in the library. Aunty Alet, my mum's cousin, flew down with me to Austin to help me shop for clothes and supplies.

Aunty had recently graduated from university and would be returning to Cameroon with her degree in hand to enter the workforce. I cried myself to sleep the first night after she left me in Austin to return to Maryland. I had many other nights that I fell asleep

with tears in my eyes but thankfully, I was less lonely once I made some new friends. I took my studies very seriously because I recognized the financial sacrifice my parents were making for my education. I did not schedule my classes around daily soap operas, I took 15 to 18 credit hours per semester and maintained a 4.0 GPA.

I transferred to the University of Maryland during my junior year to be closer to my family. I moved in with my brother Emmet and his wife, Chloe. It still tickles me when I remember the many occasions when the yellow school bus tried to pick me up as I ran to catch the university shuttle. I don't fault the driver because I could have passed for a high schooler.

Three years and nine months after arriving from Cameroon, I graduated with a degree in biology. My mother traveled from Cameroon to attend my graduation and the pride in her eyes made every sleepless night I spent studying worth it. Mummy knew I always wanted to be a physician and she pulled me aside during her trip to find out if that was still the plan. I reassured my Mum that I would apply as soon as I figured out how to pay for it, thankful that my parents had covered my undergraduate education.

A Dream Delayed But Not Denied

My first job after graduating from college was a laboratory technician getting "practical experience" in my field of study, as part of a legal immigration program. It would not be my last. As much as I loved working in the laboratory, I quickly realized that it would not pay for medical school.

I started a new job at a lab at John Hopkins University School of Public Health, a move that set me on a clear path to medical school and achieving my American dream. Opportunities opened up that were instrumental in getting my green card.

While working full-time in the lab, I enrolled in

graduate school to take advantage of the employee tuition discount but also to bolster my medical school application since I had been out of school for more than two years at the time. The work I did supported national HIV/AIDS clinical center trials. My first awareness of HIV/AIDS had occurred during my freshman year in the library.

Time Magazine had headlines about "a new disease" that was killing men in New York and San Francisco.

...and the pride in her eyes made every sleepless night I spent studying worth it

---

Here I was several years later, helping to find answers to fight this deadly disease. I am still humbled that the work I did as a young laboratory technician contributed to what is known about HIV/AIDS today.

Becoming eligible for student loans as a green card holder made attending medical school an attainable goal. I applied and was accepted into two medical schools, three months after graduating with a master's degree in health science from the John Hopkins School of Public Health.

I joined the freshman class of 1992 at Howard University in Washington, DC. and moved in once again with Emmett and Chloe, to save money, for emotional support, and the food (Chloe is a fabulous cook). I graduated on schedule with several honors.

Doctor, Wife and Mother

I got married in Cameroon one week after graduating from medical school, and my new husband joined me in Maryland two years later.

During the last year of my ophthalmology residency, I became pregnant after several in vitro fertilization cycles. My joy did not last when at 13-weeks of gestation, I started bleeding heavily while operating on a patient. I eventually lost the pregnancy.

After residency, I moved to Toccoa, Georgia and joined a multispecialty practice as a general ophthalmologist. My husband never took the job in Greenville, South Carolina as planned so I was there alone for two years. I am still in touch with Tess, one of the few friends I made during my lonely days in Toccoa.

By the time I left Georgia at the end of my contract, I had decided ophthalmology was not for me but before leaving the state, I joined the Army Reserves. I came back to Maryland and took a year off to plot my next career move.

I completed a preventive medicine residency program in June 2005 and the Army came calling. While preparing to deploy to Afghanistan a few months later, I found out I was pregnant again. My doctor recommended that I stay home because of the high risk for loss. Jell was born a few months after my fortieth birthday and has been a source of great joy and hope.

Missions, Palaces and Public Health

Two weeks after Jell's first birthday, I arrived in Baghdad, Iraq and was met at the airport by a Brigade's official who after a brief greeting, told me that the M-9 pistol I was sporting was inadequate for the duties ahead of me. I silently wondered which other deficiencies would be uncovered during the deployment. I soon became an occupant of one of Saddam Hussein's lesser palaces. Two days after landing in Baghdad, I qualified on a semi-automatic rifle.

On my first mission to Babylon, I felt lucky to snag a "window seat" on the helicopter. I quickly realized why the seat had been unoccupied as soon as we were airborne. The chopper rotors whipped the surrounding air into a cyclone that battered my face relentlessly during the entire trip. I could not speak one word and could hardly breathe. After that startling experience, I always left that seat for unsuspecting novices.

Jell

Jell's father and I divorced when he was 10 years old. The only question he asked me at the time was if his father would become his stepdad. After a brief conversation about fathers and stepfathers, he seemed satisfied. Jell continues to be a source of great joy and some of my deepest belly-laughs.

When Jell was six-years old, I called him a comedian after he said something funny. He told me emphatically "I am not a comedian; I am an American!" The poor child thought that a comedian was a person from another country, like a Canadian or even a former Cameroonian, like his mother.

Is there anything else you want the world to know about you?

I plan to start a lifestyle medicine and wellness coaching business within the next 12 months.

Who to have lunch with?

My great-grandmother, Djaratou, shr was the original immigrant in my family.

My favorite color

I love so many colors that I cannot dare to choose one.

Most Proud of...
Losing over 50 lbs, healing my chronic pain, and reversing prediabetes.

Is there anything else you would want the world to know about you?
I am an anxious introvert until I get to know you.

Short Bio
Anne Burnley, MD, MHS, MS. DipABLM, aka Dr. Ahne, is a physician, wellness strategist, and speaker. She is board-certified in Preventive Medicine and Lifestyle Medicine. Dr. Ahne is a mom to a teenage son who she is raising to be a kind human. Originally from Cameroon, she is part of a vibrant immigrant community. Dr. Ahne is passionate about public health and lifestyle medicine and loves to travel in her spare time. You can find her on Facebook: DrAhne Wellnessmd, Instagram: @dr_ahne, and on Clubhouse: @drahne

A Less Than Perfect But Blessed Life
Chinyelu E. Oraedu

GBR / NGA / USA

The Dawn of a New Day

Every immigrant has a compelling story which helps shape their life in their new country. This journey is saddled with lofty expectations and a burning desire to start life anew in a land far away from home. Embedded within this daunting venture is the desire to triumph despite all trials and tribulations. Afterall, desire is the starting point of all human achievement.

My immigrant story is like music, an arrangement of sounds with melody, rhythm and harmony, and under the right tutelage, a masterpiece is born. My life journey started in another foreign land miles away from my ancestral home in Nigeria. My parents Basil and Philo Nzeako were foreign students in Birmingham, United Kingdom in the early 1970s.

I was born on a glorious Friday in Autumn on September 26th, 1975. My big sister Dr. Ify was also born in Birmingham, a year earlier. My parents faced a lot of challenges in the United Kingdom back in those days before the world became a global village. They had no relatives or close peers who could help them with childcare or at the least offer support when needed.

They juggled their schedules despite the burden of acclimatization to the harsh winter weather with its blustery winds. By the mid 1970s, Nigeria experienced "the oil boom" and encouraged all their citizens overseas to return home. This triggered a mass return of Nigerian professionals from all over the world. My parents accepted jobs at the first indigenous Nigerian University - the University of Nigeria, Nsukka (UNN).

Nsukka is a quaint university town, tucked away in Southeast Nigeria amidst rolling hills and luscious foliage. The entire terrain is picturesque, a great sight to behold. I spent my formative years in this town and it shaped my adult life immensely. I later completed high school at one of the competitive all girls boarding unity schools in Nigeria. My desire was to attend the prestigious medical college at UNN. The heavens smiled, I was granted my heart's desire and I gained admission into the university.

My father later accepted another professorial job at the satellite campus of the University located in Enugu. Enugu is popularly known as 'the coal city', another beautiful 'hill top city' notable for its hilly geography.

By the early 1990s, life in Nigeria became unbearable, my father reluctantly made the decision to seek greener pastures in Muscat, Sultanate of Oman in the Middle East, while we stayed back in Nigeria with my mother. He visited home twice a year (Summer time and Christmas), while my mother and my younger siblings traveled to visit him more often than my elder sister and I.

This phase spanned 20 years until my father retired and returned home to Nigeria in 2015. I learned the true meaning of tenacity, sacrifice and unconditional love from my parents. Being a parent is never a burden, it is loving somebody else wholeheartedly and unconditionally, for eternity! I fondly cherish all my memories in Nigeria from my elementary days to high school and then Medical school.

Leaving the Cradle

My life in Nigeria was beautiful, I had parents who cared and provided for me and my siblings. We had many family traditions like traveling to our second home in the countryside for at least 2 weeks during

Despite all my initial disappointments, I continued to muster strength and courage...

the Christmas season. I looked forward to spending time with my elderly grandparents and numerous cousins. There were a lot of festivities during this season and you can bet my family was always decked in our flamboyant outfits. In other words, my life was enriched by my interaction with my neighbors, relatives, friends and well wishers.

Fast forward to the Summer of 2001, after my graduation from Medical school, I met and fell in love with a young man, Okey Oraedu, who was visiting Enugu from New York City, USA.

We had a lot in common; grew up in the same city, shared common interests which included our love for our families, christian faith, great intellect, good food and fashion, to mention a few. I believe the stars were aligned on that fateful day we met because I had been contemplating relocating to the UK after Medical school.

Coming to America evoked mixed emotions in me. I was happy I was beginning a new chapter in my life with Okey. Nonetheless, the idea of leaving my family scared me out of my wits. I was treading on 'uncertain and uncharted territory'.

I had to leave my family, friends, mentors, and my worldly possessions which I cherished (sounds kinda vain right?) You can imagine the emotional turmoil I experienced trying to decide which items to leave behind. Behold, this is the dilemma of some immigrants who are relocating overseas!

You work so hard in your home country to acquire worldly possessions, then end up leaving with just two 23kg suitcases and one piece of hand luggage. On arrival in America, you realize your life has been reset and rebooted to 'begin afresh'. You quickly realize that life in America is really not like it is portrayed in the posh and lush Hollywood movies. You need grit and grace!

To Be Or Not To Be?

Phew! Now the real story begins!

I felt a deep loneliness in my heart during my first few months in America. Words cannot explain how much I missed my parents and siblings. I stayed home studying and watching all the numerous soap operas on T.V. I didn't work until I started my residency in 2006. I was not 'really part of the American system', I was however considered to be part of the infamous derogatory terminology used to describe immigrants 'fresh off the boat'.

Back in those days, internet phone calls were non-existent. One had to drive to the local *"bodega"* to buy $5 calling cards that allowed you to make international calls and speak for less than 10 minutes! This was my initial welcome package. Everyone talks about the 'culture shock' new immigrants experience upon their emigration, and I experienced every bit of it.

Growing up in Nigeria, everyone looked the same. We were all different 'shades of brown'. I had a perfect family and well balanced life. The world was my Oyster. Here I was in America, voila! I felt invisible, inconspicuous, almost insignificant. *"Your name is difficult to pronounce"*, *"I will not even try to say your name"*, I heard these comments all the time. This narra-

tive stems from the perception (whether spoken or implied) that my skin color is maybe inferior therefore he/she will not even attempt to say my name.

I remember many times while sitting in the reception area waiting to be called, the feeling of trepidation knowing that your name will be 'butchered' by the caller. The moment you notice the caller, pause mid sentence, take a deep breathe or start to stutter a bit, you just rise *"that's me over here sir/ma'am"* you

> *Despite all my initial disappointments, I continued to muster strength and courage...*

respond. Despite the challenges, I never changed or shortened my given first name which in Ibo language means 'a special gift from God'.

As a newly arrived African immigrant, my hair was another albatross around my neck. Back home, I never worried about fixing my hair, or how much it cost. The rude awakening was the financial burden I incurred if I desired to always have 'perfect hair'. For someone who went to a boarding school, I never learned how to cornrow my hair and till date, this is one of my few regrets. I also quickly desensitized my

taste buds to *Naija* food and acquired new culinary interests due to the high cost of my local food at the African store.

At certain times, I reminisced about my life back in Nigeria, where I was considered 'top notch', 'pacesetter' and I really wondered whether I made the right decision to emigrate. Like they say "every cloud has a silver lining". Despite all my initial disappointments, I continued to muster strength and courage because I needed to break down barriers, educate people who ruffled my feathers and made me doubt my capability to succeed. Like it's also said, "what does not kill you makes you stronger".

Phoenix Rising

I remember telling my husband that I would not allow any negativity to dull my shine. I started charting my course, making new, purpose-driven friendships, assimilating into my adopted home. I took my US Medical Licensing Examination (USMLE) and within 2 years, I started my internal medicine residency in Brooklyn, NY with not one but two cherries on top of my cake.

I birthed fraternal twin boys Kobi and Dumeto, on Valentine's Day 2006 about four months before I started my residency training in June 2006. It was a very challenging time for me and I forever remain grateful to my sister, Dr. Ify, who helped me immensely during the first year of my training while studying for her own USMLE. My only daughter Kaira was born on March 28th, 2009. The circumstances surrounding my daughter's birth will forever remain vivid in my mind.

I was in my third year of internal medicine residency, over 35 weeks pregnant and was scheduled to take my USMLE Step 3 examination. On this fateful day, I received a frantic call from my obstetrician. He notified me about my abnormal glucose tolerance test (OGTT) and insisted I should come to the hospital for amniocentesis the same evening.

I was flustered and upset. Afterall the OGTT was done over 4 weeks ago, why did it take them so long to review the result? Results from the amniocentesis showed evidence of fetal lung maturation. The following day, after I completed the 2nd part of my examination, my husband drove me to the hospital for my caesarian section. Despite my unpreparedness, the birth of my daughter reaffirmed my inner mental toughness.

As the years have progressed, I have become more sure-footed in America, my adopted home. My husband remains a solid support in my life. The deep loneliness I felt when I came to America in July 2003 has been replaced by an immeasurable sense of happiness and contentment. The popular song by Sister Sledge, *"We are family, I got all my sisters with me"*, resonates with my current mood. I have all my 4 sisters and 1 brother currently resident in the US. We meet up during major holidays with our kids and spouses, my parents visit from Nigeria on a regular basis. Besides minor chronic ailments, my parents are healthy and

I am thankful to God for His mercy and favor. Surely, my cup is joyously overflowing.

happy and I am thankful to God for His mercy and favor. Surely, my cup is joyously overflowing.

On a personal note, my social life is fulfilling, all thanks to my wonderful circle of friends, caring church congregation at the First Presbyterian Church, Fairfield, CT and amazing neighbors.

I encourage prospective immigrants to always seek information and counsel from the right sources. Talk to people who share your "vision and mission". Avoid negativity or the naysayers. Remain humble so people will be inclined to teach or help you. Follow your intuition. Life always happens in peaks and troughs. Just like all precious natural resources, you have to dig deeper into the earth to find them.

My Mantra

There are three things I need each day. Something to look up to, another to look forward to, and the last is something I am chasing- that's my hero, the person I hope to become someday.

Favorite food

My favorite food from Nigeria is *Moi moi* (steamed bean pudding) and *Dodo* (fried plantain). These can be eaten as regular meals or comfort foods.

My Proudest Accomplishment

My decision to embark on my weight loss journey in 2019. I needed to get my mojo back. During the pandemic, I signed up with Liz, my fitness coach and she transformed my life. Within two years, I lost up to 50 pounds through dieting and regular exercise.

My Legacy

To teach my children the value of selfless service, sacrifice and charity. I believe that one can only experience true happiness by performing random acts of kindness towards the needy in our midst. I hope to someday establish a non-profit organization which provides nutritious meals to women and children in impoverished communities.

Who to thank

I would like to thank my parents Dr. Basil & Philo Nzeako for their love and sacrifice. They are true champions, they laid the solid foundation for myself and my 5 siblings.

Short Bio

Dr. Chinyelu E. Oraedu is board certified in Internal Medicine. She practices as a hospitalist in Stamford, Connecticut. She also sees patients in the outpatient setting at the pre-surgical optimization clinic affiliated with her hospital. She enjoys traveling, reading self-help books and spending quality time with her family and friends. She is very passionate about teaching people about personal finance and hopes to empower women to maintain profitable portfolios. She is married to Okey, a skilful architect and they are blessed with 3 beautiful children- twin boys Kobi and Dumeto and daughter Kaira. She can be reached at coraedu2609@gmail. com, IG: dr_chy, FB: Chinyelu Nzeako Oraedu, Clubhouse: @drchinyelu

Choosing Happiness Twice

Dr. Lulu

NGA / USA

"*You make my skin crawl*".

"*No man will ever want you*".

"*Look at you, you are as fat as a cow*" (I was 6 months pregnant.)

I smile and shake my head in disbelief every time I remember those words. Words that came out unchecked from the mouth of a man who just a few years prior, had professed his undying love for me! "*Seriously?*" My friends would ask.

"*I don't believe it*".

"He is such a calm and gentle guy".

"How is that possible?"

But it was all too possible. And all too true.

Me, Myself and my Dad!

As far back as I can remember, I'd always wanted to become an architect. I love art, I love creating and I love old buildings, until the day I had the talk with my dad. "*Why do you want to do something so masculine?*" He asked with a deep furrow on his brow. "*Who do you know that is an architect?*" "*Nne, why don't you do something a bit more feminine, like pharmacy, just like your cousin Chika?*".

I shook my 17-year-old head vigorously and declared with conviction, as my Nigerian, Igbo, red-cap chief father looked on, "*Daddy, if I must do something in the medical field, then I might as well become a doctor*". I spoke with such unwavering certainty in my voice and body language, that my poor dad caved in.

And so, the journey to my future home began. I graduated from medical school at 22. And set out for America at 26. But not before my dad counseled me to beware of drug dealers, and obsessed about my being single, then tasked me with the responsibility of raising half of my flight ticket. I raised three fourths in half the time!

America the Beautiful and the Not So...

I was bright-eyed, bushy-tailed and ready for the adventure. Full of anticipation, awe, and amazement. America!

The land *"flowing with milk and honey"*.

The land of my dreams.

The land of Howard University hospital.

H.U!

You Know!

The land of my pediatric residency.

My current home...

I couldn't wait to come to America. I wanted to experience what I had seen on the pages of *JET, Ebony* and *Essence magazines*. So, after receiving an invitation to Howard university hospital for an interview, it was on! New York! My first stop was the *"concrete jungle where dreams are made of"*! The cold snow, bright lights, smells, sounds of Brooklyn, Flatbush avenue to be exact!

Wait, what? Is this America? Is this New York? Why are the streets so dirty? Why are there so many young girls pushing baby *prams*? (I know, y'all call 'em strollers or buggies, but we call 'em prams.) Please don't

tell me they are all mothers! Where are the childrens' fathers? What's with the daily shootings and the non-stop police and ambulance sirens?

Where are the movie stars? Why can't many of the people I meet articulate a proper sentence in English? Why are they surprised that I am 26, single

---

I couldn't wait to come to America. I wanted to experience what I had seen on the pages of JET, Ebony and Essence magazines.

---

and have no kids? *"You ain't gat no kids?"* I am asked over and over, hmmm. Why do they repeatedly tell me they "like" my accent? Why can't they pronounce my four-letter last name?

And for the love of something good, where is the glove compartment in a car? Why do they call the *dustbin* a trash can, a *torch light* a flash-light, and baby *napkins*, diapers? I remember once writing an order for *Nystatin* cream to be applied to a baby's *"nappy rash"* and the commotion it caused in the newborn nursery that day (rolling my eyes).

Then I moved to Washington DC (District of Columbia, apparently, there is another Washington,

the state). I loooove downtown DC. I took the Yellow Line on the subway from my first apartment complex in Arlington, Virginia (VA) to DC. I fell in love with the historic monuments and parks. I enjoyed people-watching; the eclectic mix of humans; foreigners and locals alike. Everyone appeared to be on a mission to get somewhere ...*fast!*

Why America?

In Nigeria as in most African countries, people dream of traveling abroad, to live there. For me, my reasons were the same as those of most home-trained physicians. To make a good living doing what I love. Residency in America only takes 3 years versus 6 to 8 years in Nigeria. I also wanted to make money in dollars, so, why not?

To come to the US for residency from Nigeria, one has to take USMLE (United States Medical Licensing Examination). I took mine in Ghana (a wonderful memory). I studied for the exam with some friends and vowed to do everything in my power to pass it the first time. I think I became somewhat obsessed.

In Igboland, we say *"onye kwere, chi y'ekwere,"* meaning *"your destiny is in your hands,"* OR *"where there's a will, the universe will make a way"*. Many-a-night I sat in my father's house in Ikoyi, Lagos-Nigeria, dream-

ing about Howard University hospital. I saw myself walking the halls, wearing my white coat. I heard *"paging Dr. Umeh"* through the intercoms. I smelt and felt myself there.

Today, I can comfortably say I thought, believed and manifested myself there. Dream big or go home baby!

First Place and Tears

Living alone is not something that has ever come easy for me. As the first of six kids, the last time I lived alone was never. LOL. It turns out, I have a fear of being alone, a fear of abandonment, as my coach and I discovered recently. A fear of being with myself. A tendency to look at quietude and aloneness as *loneliness*. **A fear of solitude**.

So, I cried a lot those first few weeks and months of living in Arlington, VA. It is a suburb of DC. In the US, many people live in the suburbs of cities to avoid the hustle and bustle of downtown. Howard University is on Georgia Avenue, right in the heart of DC. It is never devoid of activity; sirens, humans, babies, pets, traffic...life. As happy as I was to live in America, I missed home. I missed the sights, sounds and smells of familiar neighborhoods, familiar streets, familiar faces. I missed my family. I missed roasted *oka* (corn) and *ube* (pear). Coming from a country where affec-

tion is typically *not* displayed through hugs or terms of endearment, I now saw that everywhere around me. As a hugger with *touch* and *time* as my top love languages, that **hurt**.

Looking back now, I wish I had taken more time to enjoy the novelty, to approach my new home and new life with more curiosity. But I didn't. Knowing what I know now about our thoughts creating our reality, I see how I easily thought myself into fear, loneliness, and sadness those early days.

As happy as I was to live in America, I missed home... I missed my family. I missed roasted oka (corn) and ube (pear).

One Sunday in particular, is etched in my memory. Since I attended a Nigerian Catholic Church, I would often dress in Nigerian garb. That day I wore *ero* and *buba* (a traditional Yoruba outfit) that had belonged to my mom.

As I walked past my full-length mirror, I caught a glimpse of my image...the person looking back at me was *mi madre!* I never knew how much alike we looked, but between that outfit and my already raw emotions, it was waterworks! I cried, and cried and cried...

I however still enjoyed my residency, made a lot of friends, learned a lot about America in general, and confirmed to myself that I had made the right decision to come to Howard, because I looooove children and being a doctor! Unfortunately, our hours as residents in those days were horrendous! We were on call every third night, leaving no time to rest, socialize or pretty much do anything else.

One other thing I had to get used to while living in northeastern United States was the winter. And Washington D.C had its' fair share of the "white stuff." One night after a particularly challenging call, I was driving home when I stepped on my brakes and got introduced to the hazardous element called "black ice". Next thing I knew, I was at the end of a four-car pile-up on NW 16th street!

Talking about hazardous events, I remember the day I stopped at a light on interstate 395 on my way home from call, only to suddenly hear what sounded like mosquitoes whining! I found myself trying to swat at the "mosquitoes" but I opened my eyes and realized the sound was actually other cars honking at me because I had fallen asleep at the wheel!

Life Afterwards
Hard to imagine how many moons ago that was!

In that time, I became a pediatrician who is about to retire from clinical medicine. I got married and divorced an emotionally and verbally abusive man. I bore 3 fine sons, currently aged 22, 20 and 16. I semi-quit clinical medicine, launched a career in public speaking, became a writing coach, and got certified as a life coach (thanks to Covid-19) and wrote three books! I am also fighting with all my might to end youth suicide.

Clarity of purpose is a phrase that eludes many, but comes easy if you allow vulnerability in.

I have learned that some people you hold dear can hurt you, and random strangers can help you. I was on the brink of death the day I filed for divorce from my ex-husband. I was also at heaven's gate the day I asked "L" to marry me. I am learning that life is what you make of it.

I now know that it doesn't take sight to reach the top, it takes vision. Clarity of purpose is a phrase that eludes many, but comes easy if you allow vulnerability in. You must denounce self-doubt and lean-in to self-belief.

While I was CEO of the largest minority-owned pediatric practice in Lancaster County, South Carolina, I met racism face to face! It will remain a clear and present danger in my life and the lives of *mis tres hijos* as long as we remain inhabitants of America, except our collective consciousness towards the word "race" changes.

I have worked hard and have lost hard.

I have laughed with janitors and sat with generals. I have owned a lot of money and filed bankruptcy. I have been actively suicidal and saved suicidal teens. As a pediatrician, I have helped bring babies into this world and have left babies to die. I have mended broken hearts and have had my own heart broken. My feelings are mine to have and I share them without reservation.

I designed and built my dream house, but realized it was not a (happy) home. I found joy in my work as a pediatrician and discovered kickboxing. I rekindled my love for writing and spoke at the United Nations, on primetime television and on a TEDx stage. I testified at the Texas statehouse and even had a stint as a lieutenant colonel and commander in the United States Air Force (ahem, I served under President Barack Hussein Obama, just to put it out there).

Not too bad for a little girl who dared to dream...

My sons are my legacy. I never leave my home without their love in my heart. I love them, but I am learning to love myself more. I now know that I can only pour into others from my overflow not from my full. While loneliness and scarcity are simply thoughts, so also are solitude and prosperity, and I choose the latter two, because, welp, I can. As I age, wisdom has come at a price, the value...priceless.

Oh, and my forever favorite color remains the boldest of reds!

Professional/Personal Motto

If you dare to *BE*lieve it, you can *absofreakinlutely BE*come it.

Who to thank

My inner child. She endured sexual assault before age 10, bullying and rape as a teen, and domestic abuse and discrimination as an adult.

Biggest mistake

Not knowing and loving myself enough...and settling.

Who to lunch with

My ancestral grandmothers on both sides, particularly the two grandmothers I knew, but missed their

funerals because I live in the diaspora. I would ask for blessings as I write the 52nd chapter of my life. I want to know how they overcame doubts. What they did when they felt lonely. What were their childhoods like? What was life like waaayyyy back then? Then, I would ask for a looooong warm hug!

Most proud of

My **V-FAB**; **V**ulnerability, **F**earlessness, **A**uthenticity and **B**oldness, even as I struggle to find them sometimes. Coming to America was a dream come true. I would do it again, and wouldn't change a thing! Life is an adventure, and I am finally settling in for the ride. I love that I have raised children who are smart, intuitive and mentally balanced. They are the best *of* me. They are the best *in* me. They will fly the Umenwaliri flag high, looong after I am gone.

Lastly...

As of the 1st of January 2021, my wife and I decided to go our separate ways after over 8 years. If anyone had told me we would not grow old together, I would never have believed them. But it was no longer working out and we "parted as friends". And while I would love to blame it all on Covid-19 or the year 2020, I know in my heart that the signs had been there all along. The vase already had cracks, the lockdown was simply the blunt force that shattered it.

One day, soon after the split, I was on the phone with my eldest offspring, crying and pouring my heart out to them. After listening to me for a while, they asked, *"Mom what are you afraid of?"* I sucked in my snort and whispered, *"I don't want to be the woman who is divorced twice"*. Without missing a beat, I heard my child, my beloved young adult's voice respond with, *"Mom, what if you are the woman who chooses happiness twice?"*

Short Bio

Dr. Lulu aka The Momatrician, is a board-certified Pediatrician and a mom. But in her spare time, she is also a bit of this, that, and others. The "others" include embracing being an immigrant physician, and a Nigerian in the Diaspora. She is a speaker, podcaster, blogger, suicide prevention activist and life coach.

She helps parents of LGBTQ+ kids accept, understand and support their LGBTQ+ kids. She also coaches speakers and helps would-be authors overcome their fears of speaking and writing respectively. Find her on social media: IG; @ askdoctorlulu; Twitter; @uchennaumeh9, Facebook; Dr-Lulu, Clubhouse; Dr.Lulu(She/Her). Email coach@ dr-lulu.com For appointments; calendly.com/drlulu, website; www.dr-lulu.com Tel: 802-768-1180.

Awele: The Favored One

Ebere Azumah

Sweet Sixteen

"A dream is a wish our hearts make when we are awake and asleep." ~ Dr. Ebere Azumah

For several reasons, some dreams come true while others are stillborn. I am the fourth of six children. By the age of 13, I knew exactly what I wanted to be. A lawyer! A bold and fearless one who will serve and protect the innocent. I believe I would have made a great lawyer. I really do.

Millions of Africans and Non-Africans dream to live in America to provide better lives for themselves and their families. They pray and hope for this dream to come true, after all, "America is the land of opportunity."

Believe it or not, I prayed and hoped for that too. One day, my prayer was answered! "We are going to America! We got our visas!" My eldest brother shouted excitedly as I picked up the telephone.

Oh, I remember that day like it was yesterday! It was the start of something beautiful; a new journey for me especially. I had so many dreams about my life in America. You see, our mother hoped for a better future for her six children. When she didn't manifest her dream in Nigeria, it motivated her to relocate to America, leaving us behind.

I was young, but understood it was a difficult decision for her to make. My siblings and I were saddened by her absence, but we prayed to be reunited with her someday. After years of separation, we were finally going to be with our mother, and become a part of the American dream. I was also excited to be celebrating my sweet 16 birthday in America!

It is a big deal in America!

On February 6, 1998, I was breathing the same air as the people in Metro-Detroit, Michigan. The temperature was brutally unfriendly in the winter period, but we were dressed for it. Our flight from Lagos, Nigeria, was 16 hours and 30 something minutes long with a layover in Amsterdam.

I am thankful it was an uneventful flight. My mother was at the airport before our plane landed. Her face lit up upon seeing her babies, and her heart was as full as ours. "Wow! I am in America!" I thought, as my heart did a breakdance with a big smile different from my freezing face. After a short drive in her new minivan, we pulled up in front of our new home, a beautiful townhouse in Taylor, Michigan.

She had cooked lots of food and there were also lots to drink too. My mother then introduced us to some of her close friends, neighbors, and our relatives in the area. There I met two of my cousins who ended up mentoring me as I navigated through the American school system. We celebrated and gave thanks to God.

My first experiences in America were interesting. Stepping on an escalator for the first time was strange, yet exciting! A moving staircase? Panicking that an elevator would crash each time I got on it, or that the lights would go off, were real issues I am so thankful I overcame.

My first day of high school was peculiar as I observed my new classmates while they observed me. Very weird indeed! I really loved school, however, moving from one classroom to another was exhausting, but I eventually got the hang of it. Before I knew it, the school bell rang, and it was time to go home.

I got on the bus but did not realize that my brother was not on it. When the bus started to move, I saw him running after it. I was freaking out without

I am an Igbo woman from the Igbo tribe of Nigeria

the other students or the driver noticing that I was. Feeling different, weakened my courage to speak up. The bus kept moving and my poor brother gave up. I watched him watch the bus with his shoulders and head down.

My heart was totally broken!

I was so afraid of my mother's reaction. In our Igbo culture, we are expected to care for our siblings, especially in a foreign land where your only support system is your family. I could have opened my mouth and asked the bus driver to stop, but I didn't. I couldn't. I was not a shy teen. I am an extrovert, but being the

"new kid on the block" completely crippled me right there on the bus.

My heart was saying what my lips should have been saying, but they were not moving. When I got home, I called my mom at work to inform her. She was not happy about it as I expected. I cried and cried, praying for my brother to return home safely. Thankfully, the school found a way to bring him home. Afterwards, my mother did not fail to re-educate me on the importance of family and being fearlessly bold.

After several weeks in America, I was starting to get used to the weather and loving my new school. I even started to make new friends. BeLinda and Jacinta were in some honors classes with me. We were one of the few minority students in AP classes. Eventually, we became great friends. At the time, I had no idea we were minorities. Heck! I didn't understand color! I only understood tribes.

I am an Igbo woman from the Igbo tribe of Nigeria. Although I grew up in Jos, Plateau State in the northern region of Nigeria, and barely visited the south east where my patrilineal gene is from. However, in America, I was classified as just a Black woman. This identity was totally new to me; maybe because I was not taught the transatlantic slavery history in school back in Nigeria.

My Immigrant Pride

Attending Harvard was one of my biggest goals and accomplishments! In May 2014, I had just graduated from my rigorous Ob/Gyn residency and was going to become an attending physician. Walking down the make-shift stage and giving a speech, I was grateful that my studying years were over.

My desire to become a physician was cultivated by Ms. Eva, my third-grade teacher in Jos. One day after class, she pulled me aside and said, "Ebere, you should consider a career in medicine. You are great in science." But I had always wanted to become an attorney like Matlock! You know, the television show?

After three years as an attending, I knew I wanted to learn more about public health, health disparities, and how to create a community education curriculum. So, I applied to Harvard T. H. Chan School of Public Health. It was the only school I applied to and fortunately got accepted into. I felt so favored.

For years I had dreamed that I would one day become an alumnus of one of the best institutions in the world, and I have. When you have a dream, don't just pray about it; work towards it, believe in yourself, and have faith.

Who doesn't have a story? Tell me. Who? Yes, we all have a story; more than one story to tell about our lives and our experiences. I know I was born to not only exist, but to live wholly and fulfill my life's purpose(s). Challenges are meant to strengthen us, and not break or weaken us. We go through experiences because life is designed to be that way. The keyword here is "through," meaning that no challenge or season is permanent.

I am grateful for my strong Christian faith. It helped me to overcome the pain of change, especially when I was in a fiery car accident in 2014 that left me with over 30% skin burns. Sometimes, I forget I have the scars when I wear my long sleeve shirts or dresses. I could have died that night, but grace found me, and I survived. The grace of God remains ever sufficient in my life.

I know the pain I dealt with, but my faith in God, the love of my family especially from my brother and my dreams carried me through that season. Believe it or not, through my pain, I developed the skills and strength to live fully and joyfully. Unbeknownst to me, these skills now guide me to help myself and others to succeed and to dream big.

After surviving my accident, I realized even more that God loves me and still needs me on earth to carry out His will. You can call me *Awele*, which in Igbo language means "the highly favored one."

Quotes That Inspire Me

I have several quotes that guide and empower me, but these three are exceptional. One is my personal quote, *"I embrace positivity and shun negativity."* I agree, *"Tough times never last, but tough people do."* Sometimes, I am scared of my dreams; big dreams, but this third quote constantly motivates me to *"just do it"*. I remember being scared when I decided to co-found Love Your Menses, Inc. with Bria Gadsden; turning a non-profit event that was started in Boston into a global organization. *"Just Do It!"*

Every day, I work very hard to be the best of me and to live my best life. So, how I feel and look matter to me. It's not vanity. It's called self-love. When you love yourself, you should also care for yourself. Self-care is needed to function and reboot. Otherwise, we break down. I categorize self-care to target the spiritual, emotional, physical, and educational areas of my life. I always make time to meet these needs.

On a regular basis, I eat healthy, learn something new that is necessary for my self development, and I reach out to someone special to check on them and to catch up, to mention a few. A fellow Life Coach and my friend, Dr. L D, used recharging our cellphones as an analogy to recharging ourselves. Think about it, and you know it's true. But wait! You shouldn't allow your

'battery' to start running low to know that you need to rejuvenate your body, mind, and spirit.

Unapologetically Authentic

Sometimes, our lives might seem imperfect in a traditional sense, but individually, we know it's just perfect for us. No matter where you were born or come from, no matter where you live, always be and do your best. I love Amanda Gorman's quote, *"There is always light, if only we're brave enough to see it. If only we are brave enough to be it."* Therefore, I live my best life, no matter the challenges that may come my way. I am a woman, an Igbo woman, a Black woman...unapologetically authentic. I am fierce, strong, a victor, fun, bold, humble, brave, kind, transparent, and unstoppable [in Christ] because I am highly favored by His grace.

What legacy would you like to leave behind?

I hope that my daughter and sister will understand who I am and carry on the baton and become advocates for girls and women.

What is your personal or professional motto?

Flowing Life Unapologetically, this is actually the Love your Menses, Inc. motto but I take this comment seriously and hope many women will learn to flow in their lives unapologetically. Sometimes, because of what people will say, we dampen our shine so we don't offend others. But this motto says, why not shine?

Is there anything else you would want the world to know about you?

I would want the world to know that I became who I am because of my struggles and experiences navigating the world as an unconventional woman in America.

What is my favorite food from my home country?

I have an eclectic taste in food, this makes it difficult to pick one particular food.

Who is the one person in my life that I would like to thank?

I would love to thank my mom. She is a strong woman that worked hard to create a better life for her family. Her passion for improving things sometimes made her to be misunderstood but always appreciated.

Short Bio

Ebere Azumah, MD, MPH, ACC, FACOG is a board-certified Obstetrician and Gynecologist, trained DONA Doula with an interest in high-risk Obstetrics, Perinatal Anxiety, and Mood Disorders. She is also a Certified ICF Life Coach, Organizational Consultant, Professional Speaker, Social Entrepreneur, Author, Blogger, Public Health Expert with a focus on community education. She is the Co-Founder and President of Love your Menses, Inc. and the Founder of Healthy and Uplifted Platform, a branch of her company Azumah Solutions LLC, for which she is the Founder and Chief Executive Officer.

Jisike - Morning is Nigh

Ijeoma Too-Chiobi

For a moment, my joy knew no bounds as I received the news of relocating to the United States. Then came the sleepless nights and racing hearts. Is it a worthy adventure? Who do I know, do I leave my job, my family? Endless questions. "God show me your plan for me", I often prayed. He sure has a wry sense of humor. Prayer was answered. How? I was laid off. Then the relocation plans, selling off some of our assets and informing family and friends. February 29th was the D-day; cries, hugs, pictures.

This story is told from the colors that radiate - yellow and orange - colors of EMPOWERMENT. Relocated with my young family of four; husband, three-year-old daughter, and a one-year-old son. We moved in with a family for two months while searching for an apartment. Where could we get an apartment without a credit history? Finally, we were blessed with an apartment. A donation of our first bed, naturally, went to the children while the floor provided good nights' sleep for my husband and I.

The struggles were real. Sharing a car, waking the children up in the middle of the night to either drop off or pick up one of the parents from work was interesting to say the least. Breakage into the apartment - children's snacks were stolen, 911 was called thrice, they are yet to find the address.

What about walking the aisles in a store looking for biscuits and directed to the frozen food aisle, alas, should have said cookies and not biscuits. Then came tumbling down new vocabulary – lines for queues; candy for sweets, soda for mineral...

A Rank, Not Mine
Yeah, within the first month, I joined the United

States Navy but had to ask to be honorably discharged because I was not given a rank that matched my educational qualifications as the recruiter had promised. The little money we had was quickly depleting as we were maintaining a car and paying for an apartment and other bills. Not finding the sort of job I had set my eyes on was stressful.

Stress invited its cousins - depression and doubt. Did we make the right decision? No room for second-guesses, we have a young family to feed. What next? Initiation into this new world began with my first job at a salad bar. An unlikely job for someone who doesn't like to cook. The job's demanding schedule was too much to bear, and when I cut my finger about two weeks in, I decided it was time to quit.

Propellers

Job searches and college applications happened simultaneously. I was admitted to study pharmacy at one of the universities, but the household needed a steady income, so I defaulted to my childhood career aspiration - education. Was getting into the teaching field easy? Nope. It was not without its disappointments.

Waiting for the completion of the certification program did not translate to folding my arms and staying home with bills to be paid. So, I got a position as a long-term substitute teacher in a behavior classroom; was I scared out of my skin when one of my students came to school with a gun after breaking into a home? You bet. On the move again.

It's not over till you quit. Getting a teaching appointment was not without its share of frustrations; one that comes to mind was at a job fair where one of the recruiters commended my qualifications but commented, "I am not sure that the students will

Initiation into this new world began with my first job at a salad bar.

understand your accent". Thank God finally, I got a job. Enrolling into school and at the same time working two jobs to make ends meet. Breathing sighs of relief - thanks to the innocence of the students that helped me with certain pronunciations.

I recall one instance, a student asked me for an eraser and in my thick accent I said "ask your neighbor". She was so confused. I could hear her mutter repeatedly "neighbor", the way I said it, she was trying to make out what that word meant. Salvation came when the student sitting next to her leaned-in and whispered, "I think she means neighbor" in her American accent.

I toyed with the new pronunciation in my brain and when I felt comfortable, I proceeded to ask the student, "were you able to get the eraser from your neighbor?", this time practicing the pronunciation of the word, the student beamed and said "yes". I began re-learning word pronunciations for the benefit of my students. When I recall such moments, I laugh out loud.

Then, I became aware of the concept of special education for the first time. It was regarded as a critical area because of the shortage of teachers in this field. The school district offered stipends for teachers in this field. I was drawn in not because of the stipend, although that didn't hurt, but out of curiosity, as special education was not popular in my time in Nigeria. I embraced the field in its entirety leading to my becoming an educational diagnostician – evaluating children's needs by diagnosing learning delays and customizing their educational plans – as I wanted to dissect the brains of the students with disabilities to understand their unique learning processes. Interesting and informing it was.

Then came a need to shift from gear two to three. Disappointments and rejections, rather than being impediments, were propelling. Yes, you guessed it right because I met with another propeller. As the

2014/2015 Educator of the Year, the time was right for an assistant principal position at a school that I was a foundation staff. A reply by the principal that I would not be invited for an interview led to yet another glorious decision to explore the field of mental health, graduating with a 4.0 GPA from the renowned Texas A & M University, San Antonio, Texas.

The next personal challenge is SHHH, curbing my sweet tooth. I am yet to win this fight. In the spirit of sportsmanship, I accept not winning each competition. I am not giving up on this now that it's been publicized.

I could not complete this story without thanking my propelling factors – the people who did *not* believe in me because they made me work even harder, and the people who, despite my shortcomings believed in me – my spouse, Tochukwu Chiobi aka Baba Toks, the wind beneath my wings; my children Lummy, Al, Usosa, and Esom. Some great people who made remembering my immigrant status a non-issue. Yemisi, a friend since 2000 - quite instrumental to my sanity; a ready shoulder to cry on.

Maintaining sanity comes in different forms like taking walks around my neighborhood, hitting the gym, or simply talking about it. Self-affirmation quotes come in handy. Playing solitaire is simply IT.

Many humans believe in higher powers, I am not different. Being a Catholic, you can count on almost always catching me with a ROSARY. I do not leave the house without morning prayers and blessing my household.

I am continuously reminding myself that life's struggles may not be won just by my powers alone. I sometimes ponder picking the brains of some persons like the Blessed Virgin Mother. I am curious to know her immediate reaction to the angel's proclamation; how she processed the news and at what point she came to terms with the proclamation?

Life has its fair share of challenges, uncertainties, and surprises. Hardly anything in life is cast in stone. Wherever or whatever I am now does not indicate where or what I would be tomorrow. It is great to have a dream, to believe it and chase it with grit and dexterity. Nobody can define you if you do not permit them, neither is it the right of that person to validate you. Do not get me wrong, people are entitled to their opinion(s) of you; however, you do not need to feed into that opinion.

What is your personal or professional motto?
Guide and/or teach people how to treat you. Do things that please you provided you are not intentionally

hurting others. The right person will navigate towards you. Keeping my dreams real and acknowledging the steady and gradual progress towards the big picture has always worked for me as well as expunging all forms of negativity. Expectations have no limit. Reach a goal, achieve it, then set another; shattering those glass ceilings one after the other. DO NOT BE AFRAID OF MAKING NEW MISTAKES.

I have made my share of mistakes. And old ones shouldn't hold me back from making new mistakes. Yikes, should I let y'all into this mistake? I guess I can!!! At about the age of seventeen, I attended the traditional marriage of one of my cousins where all sorts of drinks were available. Nigeria, at that time, did not have an age requirement for alcohol consumption. Bottles of Mateus Rosé wine were on the table I shared with my cousins. My sweet tooth got in the way and I had my fill till my body felt out of this world.

With ceilings spinning, I felt I was passing out until a cousin sought me out and informed me that I was intoxicated. After that experience, I made a decision to stay away from alcoholic beverages when not in the comfort of my home.

Life experiences help form ideologies, philosophies, and mottos which are fluid. At all times in my life, my motto is '*rejection is the propelling wind beneath my wings*', and my personal motto is: "*Cherish life. Whatever comes my way is for a reason*".

If you could thank one person in your life (living or dead) who would it be and why?
Even though my journey to America didn't start with me chasing that dream, I am glad that I came back to education where I continually touch the lives of others more than I had envisioned. I did as a teacher,

Expectations have no limit. Reach a goal, achieve it, then set another; shattering those glass ceilings one after the other.

as an educational diagnostician, and now as a mother, friend, professional school counselor, and mental health professional.

The one person I will thank are my parents – oops that's definitely not one person. The one person then would be my mother - a beacon of hard work, a high school French teacher, who at the same time traded in house decorations, fish and apparels, to supplement her household income. My mother taught me the economics of managing a home; I doubt that I am making an A in that, but I surely learned a lot from my

PRECIOUS GEM who comes second to none. She did all of that with humility while remaining steadfast to her love of God.

What legacy would you like to leave behind?
Having experienced life in two different continents is a plus, first I take the task of being the primary role model for my biological children as sacrosanct. Working towards set goals despite the odds and never accepting less, is the legacy I hope to leave for my children and those our paths cross.

What is your favorite food from your home country?
Nigeria boasts of amazing healthy dishes making it difficult to have a favorite. If suya could be considered as "food" then I would be my favorite. I salivate as I write this because I am visualizing various dishes that are presently out of my reach.

Is there anything else you would want the world to know about you?
Cognizant of the fact that I am originally from Nigeria, it is my ultimate ambition to extend the American educational perspective to Nigeria with emphasis on reworking public education for children with disabilities. In my time, counseling was not offered in public schools. However, it is heartwarming to know that this is no longer the case.

It is my desire to utilize my acquired educational skills and tools to positively contribute to the educational reform in Nigeria someday. Educational reform is always a work-in-progress and may rightly differ in different countries. Nonetheless, it is expedient for us to continue to be open-minded in exploring innovative ideas in this domain. Relocating to the United States still has its worthwhile challenges. Hence, I am still here by choice.

Short Bio
Ijeoma Too-Chiobi - Licensed Professional Counselor (LPC), Professional School Counselor, educator, mother, wife, friend. Life is what one chooses to make out of it. Live life to the fullest, be bold and make those mistakes. As a mental health therapist, I am happy to walk the walk and empower the clients. I love to eat and sleep, weird huh?

In the Promised Land

Judith Obatusa

NGA / CAN

As I entered the aisle, she was a couple of feet away. She looked up and our eyes met. Mine lit up with recognition but she looked right through me like she had never seen me before. I was shocked and confused. As I walked towards her, she turned and walked away. I wondered what I had done to make her act that way.

As I stepped up to the sidewalk in front of my son's school, I saw her. "What a pleasant surprise!" I thought, "We have children in the same school." With a wide smile on my face, I walked towards her to say hello. When I got to her side, she totally ignored me and turned towards the road, as if to avoid me. Every time we met, even in school meetings, she never acknowledged me.

These women were staff in some of the settlement programs I was participating in. They were some of the first people I met when I arrived in Canada in 2012.

C.A.N.A.D.A

I remember the day we received the email that we should proceed to the embassy with our passports for our permanent residency visa to Canada. This was an answer to prayers and the culmination of a process which started four and half years earlier.

This long-awaited news came with a two-month deadline, exactly two weeks after my baby's fourth birthday. "Be in Canada on or before July 30th or lose your visa and begin the process from scratch."

So, the scramble began.

The decision to come to Canada was not one that I had made for myself. I was not overly enthusiastic about migrating because I believed one could succeed wherever they lived as long as they were upright and hardworking. Coming to Canada was something my husband really wanted and he worked quite hard to make it a reality. I remember telling him to focus on something else exactly four years after we began the process. Being the man of few words that he is, he said nothing to me but continued fasting and praying about it. I must say the man had faith!

Whenever the question, "why Canada?" was posed to me, my answer was always "To give my children a better life" but in hindsight, I was truly only following my husband.

The only thing about giving our children a better life is that we never really asked our children how they felt about it. We had lofty dreams of our new life but never envisaged the acculturation challenges we would face settling in Canada.

Me and the "Isms"
Behind the smooth roads, constant electricity, great WiFi and the novelty of living in the "promised land", we did not put much thought into the cultural differences and those intangible but dear connections we were leaving behind in Nigeria.

According to some of those I asked, staff at the settlement classes were not allowed to befriend me because I was their client. So, many of the first people I met in my community pretended they did not know me when they met me out and about.

I must say that I was a "well colonized" woman when we arrived because somewhere in my subconscious, I believed that the "White man" was a person of integrity who always had the best interest of others in their words and actions.

Though it seemed the playing field was equal in Canada, I experienced racism concealed in microaggressions, classism and otherism. The most shocking of all, was that it was also coming from some fellow migrants of colour (MOCs).

We had lofty dreams of our new life but never envisaged the acculturation challenges we would face...

Some MOCs that had been in Canada for a longer time treated new immigrants in a condescending manner and sometimes ridiculed their newbie status. The concept called "I better pass my neighbour syndrome" in Nigeria, where people act superior to others because they believe they are better than them, was alive and well even in Canada, "the promised land".

Being the trusting "colonizee" that I was, it took me a couple of years after arriving in Canada to finally come to terms with the fact that whether White,

Black and any colour in between, we are all human and among humans can be found the fiend, fake and YES, flawed.

Thankfully, despite the "isms", there were many organizations and individuals that invested resources into empowering immigrants like me to succeed.

Lost Baggage

In life, we move with our baggage, both physical and emotional. Mine showed up in how I saw myself. I arrived in Canada with a Bachelor degree, 14 years experience in marketing communications, my bags of beans and Indomie noodles, and a suitcase packed full with feelings of inadequacy. To make matters worse, exactly four weeks after I arrived in Canada, my father and only living parent passed away suddenly.

His death completely destabilized me and I lost my *raison d'etre* for desiring success. The suffering I endured from this loss was so great that for the next one year, I could barely put one foot in front of the other. I merely existed for my children. As I grieved my loss, I finally came to the realization that I had become an orphan.

The day my father was buried, I was in a settlement

class at the New Canadians' Centre of Excellence. Thankfully, a classmate whom I had mentioned this to, asked permission for the class to observe one minute of silence in his memory. Besides this, no one, including myself, actually really acknowledged my pain. My father died and, so did my zest for life.

Eventually, love came to the rescue.

To Leave or to Lift?

When my older children's struggles with systemic racism in the school system threw me into the net of the child welfare system and the stigma and discrimination that came with it, I had to choose whether to lift my children or leave them to the wiles of the system.

I chose to lift my children. I chose to love on them and brand them with a love so deep that no matter the darkness they faced, the light of that love would always shine through. This choice brought me out of the doldrums of grief and I signed up for the Local Employment Connection (LEC) program offered by Women's Enterprise Skills Training (WEST).

The 2014 LEC program changed my life. It challenged my feelings of inadequacy by showcasing my strengths. Whatever shame I was advised to feel about being involved with the child welfare system,

by those I thought knew better, was overwhelmed by the new future LEC helped me see.

LEC provided skilled immigrant women with all round support - professional, community and personnel - to help them settle in Canada successfully. There were career personality tests, writing coaching, clothes and fashion tips, certifications, networking events, internships to get our feet wet in the Canadian workforce and job search help.

Judithmusing

Grief had dried up my desire to write but our writing coach, Mary Anne Adam, encouraged me to revive my writing because I had a gift. A gift, Judith! This was something new. So, I revived my blog - *JudithMusing*

Frank Abbruzzese encouraged us to set up twitter accounts, so I made my twitter debut and haven't looked back. I didn't think I was any good at using digital software but after Susan Snively's classes where I passed all three Microsoft certifications, I became more confident.

Bonnie Naccarato and Olusola Taiwo guided us to networking events. The late Joanna Parris, Windsor's Etiquette Nanny, schooled us on how to conduct ourselves in these spaces and also organized a professional photoshoot for our profile headshots.

Lillian Gallant and other LEC team members, began the WEST Toastmasters club. Six months after I joined, I was top three in a speech contest. Every step of the way, the LEC team helped us and celebrated us. Their invaluable support greatly improved my self-confidence.

The Tapestry of My Life

Even as a skilled immigrant, the lack of Canadian schooling and work experience was an albatross that one carried until they found someone to give them a leg up. WEST's LEC was the leg-up for me.

I met Becky Parent through LEC and chose to do my program internship with her at Leadership Windsor Essex. She helped me see how not having Canadian education or experience could not stop my contributions to making the world around me better. This opportunity opened up new relationships that led me to two of my best friends in Canada - Lisa Raffoul and Noah Tepperman.

Mary Aganze, a fellow LEC participant, told me I would be a good fit for a program she had recently completed in Trios College. The college told me that a Canadian credential evaluation and a copy of my transcript was all I needed - no need to send for my transcript from Nigeria, a painful process best avoided.

Eureka! I could find a Canadian University that would accept the same. Voila! Royal Roads University (RRU)! I applied and got accepted into the Master of Arts in Intercultural and International Communication (MAIIC) program. This was right up my alley!

The RRU experience was one of those self esteem building opportunities that help you discover your potentials and bring your best to the fore.

I completed my Masters degree in March, signed the offer for a great job in British Columbia on my birthday, April 29th, convocated in June and resumed work in July 2019 at a place where I am wanted and appreciated.

Though my settlement challenges were numerous and even traumatic, my inherent belief in the goodness of humanity led me to people who bolstered my strength and stood with me as I navigated the sometimes treacherous paths of life in the promised land.

We are all connected in a tapestry of relationships. To be successful as an immigrant or even as a person, one needs to recognize that everyone we meet is a thread with which the tapestry of our life is woven.

What is your personal or professional motto?

Never give up because all things - hard things, sad things, bad things - are working together for your good. If you look closely for learnings in your trials, you will discover your testimony.

What legacy would you like to leave behind?
A legacy of love. True love is not an emotion but an action. It is not a passion but a decision. It is not a sprint but a marathon. True love is not given in short brilliant bursts but in an enduring blaze. My son once told me that I love hard. That's the legacy I want to leave - A woman who loved hard through tribulations and triumphs.

If you could thank one person in your life (living or dead) who would it be and why?
My Lord Jesus. His life and death epitomize love. Because he came to earth and walked in my shoes, he feels my pain and strengthens my heart to surmount every challenge I encounter. Because he died to pay the price for the deliverance of those who rejected Him, I know that I can keep loving those He brings my way even when it is difficult.

What is your favorite food from your home country?
Pounded yam and native okra soup. My favourite food from my home country used to be fried rice and chicken but now that pounded yam has become a nov-

elty, it has changed. Native okra soup is made with chopped okra and spices.

Is there anything else you would want the world to know about you?
Success in anything does not come by chance. You must first decide your goal and then pursue that goal to the very end. Know that as soon as you decide your goal, there will be many distractions along your way but decide to not give up.

I want to encourage every immigrant reading this book to know that though the road may be bumpy and the journey long, if you hang in there, you will yet enjoy your promised land.

Short Bio
Judith Obatusa - Ardent, Benevolent and Spunky - is a Nigerian-Canadian who is passionate about de-stigmatizing immigrant acculturation challenges amongst migrants of colour. She 'shamelessly' shares her personal struggles with domestic violence and the child welfare system in Canada to empower others and help them succeed in their promised land. She lives in Greater Vancouver and is mother to four great nations. In her spare time, she enjoys worshipping God, serving in the community, reading, writing, cooking and creating positive memories with her children.

Oh! Happy Days!

LyndaU

NGR

Once upon a time, there was this little girl who dreamt many nights about what the world looked like from her bedroom window. Such dreams, a lot of the time, back in the day, were viewed as 'useless' thoughts of a little girl who had nothing better to do.

In fact, one night she was caught, sitting out on the lower-rooftop of the house in the wee hours of the night; well at the time, it didn't seem like that big of a deal, but to her auntie who had the misfortune of seeing her out there that night, it was deemed "a communion with the spirits".

Questions came flooding in. Assumptions made.

She confused, not understanding what the fuss was about.

The gavel came down.

The spirits had acquired her soul!

I am having such a good hard laugh now, remembering their faces, when the rest of the household saw or heard about my 'escapade' on the rooftop. Anyway, that was me dreaming until those dreams became a reality when I got older and had a good paying job. Then my adventure began!

I see myself more of a sojourner than an immigrant in the sense that I have never felt I can live anywhere else outside my home country, Nigeria. So, I sought to travel; to visit, to tour, rather than to settle. Oh, happy days! I was so proud of the fact that I could at any point in time, have the capacity and ability to visit any part of the world that would have me.

I loved my life. I still do. Many times, I chose the countries and locations from a simple map. I saw myself as a 'Jenny Walker' in the flesh...those little-girl-dreams were becoming a reality and I was doing it all by myself.

In many ways, I have had a sensational life. I was never that one you called 'the brain' in my younger days. However, as I grew older, I realized that being academically sound with plenty of the 'streets' in me, would be the winning combination I needed to succeed. And succeed I did.

"I see things in colours," I tell people. Maybe this informed my choice of painting as my first degree. I often over-analyse challenging situations as they affect me. When I was younger, I addressed my challenges with sheer doggedness but by my early 30s, I discovered how powerful prayer was in resolving my matters.

Finding myself in my first corporate job opened my eyes and mind to God's goodness through prayer. I quickly discovered, early in my professional life that giving up was never an option, especially because I was primarily in a male-dominated industry. Therefore, NO, though a complete sentence, was not acceptable when I faced difficult clients. Nor was it acceptable in the face of strenuous tasks, or a condescending immigration officer or really, anybody in a host country I am visiting.

Until the outbreak of COVID19, I traveled. I would go to local places, or take a short trip to sister African countries when I needed to get away. To clear my head I would simply jet off because I was due for an out-of-town 'waka'. So far, I have been to 17 countries on 4 of the 7 continents of the world, including the Vatican City.

It was such a thrilling experience to have been only 2 feet away from the Pope himself – powerful, emotional, in reverence.

While it might seem like a lot to some, I feel I haven't scratched the surface of what's out there to be explored. In those moments when I self-criticize, I'd check how many of my trips I'd made with a partner I was romantically involved with and I must say it came up to about 3%, only. So I guess I am not one for heavy lifting, dramatic traveling or luggage carrying. I just do me.

Some of the countries I have visited were work related, however I never missed the chance to discover her people, food – I am very adventurous when it comes to food, her tourist sites and ancient places if any. The one place my jaw dropped in shock of their kind of food was in the Republic of Iran. I was served, and ate plain white rice with berries! Yup, just small-sized red berries.

Then another memorable trip was my first time in Dubai, in the early 2000s, way before the craze consumed Nigerians, I had the privilege of being hosted for 4 nights at the Burj Al Arab; that was the most breathtaking hotel I have ever seen or been in. Half a 10 Euro note and half a 5 Euro note came home with me because we made a promise that if we did meet again, anywhere in the world, those notes will be together and so will we. Noel. I still carry them in my wallet...

Oh! Happy days!

Mumbai in India, was so similar to Lagos, Nigeria, in terms of population size versus land and residential space. The ever present sharp contrast between the rich and the poor was palpable. But the food! Oh my! I loved their dishes so much so that I made a list of various spices to take home and try out. The butter Naan bread? To die for.

All I know is that I am not what or who I planned I was going to be nor did I even attempt to be who my parents wanted me to be, when asked 'what do you want to become when you grow up?'. I had planned to be famous, but alas! I am a simple single mother working as hard as any to make things work for me and my one and only.

The one thing I was sure of was that I was going to see the world.

So, imagine me, *'ajala the traveller'*, without a mobile phone with a camera! How would my journeys have been captured? How would I have stored all of them beautiful memories of the picturesque road trips and sunsets in different time zones? I have praised and thanked God for the inventors of the mobile phone because it has become a very essential appendage. For me, a mobile phone is definitely much more than a communication device!

The world is such an open book, all one needs to do is choose your blank page and begin your story. The adage "if life throws you lemons, make lemonade" is so apt about how one should approach life. We were

Holding my own in a room has always given me great joy...

created for a reason, that reason we may never know until we begin our journey.

Even Jesus encountered challenges and grave temptations, so who are we not to experience ours? However, we can always do better than our bad neighbour by showing and sharing love. I stand for what I believe in and I never let anyone tell me I can't be who or do what I think will make me happy.

In my travels, I have encountered a host of people, from those who had the *"How did she get here?"* look, to

"Who does she think she is?" body language. I always identify these traits and either engage to correct those global perceptions or I walk away; actually more like, live to fight another day.

Holding my own in a room has always given me great joy and improved my confidence and as such I admire quite a number of women who have done the same on a global scale. As a matter of fact, I admire all such strong women doing great things within their space, on a macro and micro level.

I would absolutely love to touch lives, impact positively and change a greater percentage of how women are viewed, perceived and treated, most especially how African women are experienced by the world. A great starting place would be the boardroom.

Had I taken certain opportunities at the time they were presented to me, I believe I would be making those positive effects from the boardroom now. It is important that young people realize that, despite the choice(s) they make for their future, they can talk their parents through it. All our parents need is to understand why, see us actively chasing that dream and they'd be fine. I say this because there was this one opportunity to work and live abroad I never pursued, thinking my parents would never buy into it, oh, how wrong I was!

Anyway that's that about that and life has since then thrown me more than my fair share of lemons and I have responded very well by making many flavours of lemonade – even rebranded the lemons as my way of owning them!

My legacy

Invest wisely. Invest from your very first salary. Don't wait until you have 'enough money', there is not one time when this will happen. Guess what? That investment is what will make you more money. Then use that money to help as many people as you can. Don't wait until you have 'plenty more'! I believe in the law of Karma either good or bad.

Motto NO is not an acceptable answer.

Thankful message

I will always thank God because HE gave me everything I have now and has already planned how my future will be. HE ultimately has brought into my life all those who have been instrumental in shaping me; those who stay a while and those who are still doing what God has designed them to do in my life. By the way, I consider myself more spiritual than religious, just in case you were wondering, wonder no more.

Food? What about it?

No favourite food. Instead I have a host of 'loves'... like Jollof rice with dodo, then my ultimate poison, boiled-fried yam with fried eggs/egg sauce. Nigerian traditional foods are mostly soups with swallows, toh! I am not a soup nor swallow person, so I am out!

What else is there about LyndaU?

Well, it depends on which set of eyes are gawking for that information. I am but human, a woman.

With bright, expectant eyes,

A warm heart and colorful dreams.

She's open to awesome possibilities

Taking advantage of those slices of hope set before her. Doesn't judge her actions too harshly. Pats her shoulder whenever the light switches from amber to green, As she says, "I owe myself a good YES".

Remember that NO, though a complete sentence, doesn't mean it's all over, instead flip it into a paragraph.

Walk away if it gets murky. Don't sweat it!

There is always another cup to fill.

Stay safe but stay strong and keep pushing yourself towards your El Dorado - yours, not anyone else's!

The life is yours.

The dreams are yours.

The hope is yours.

The steps are yours.

The results will be yours.

The joy will be shared, buh it's yours.

Stay true. Stay honest. Be good.

One more thing, don't be a stranger to your Creator; immerse yourself, it's rewarding

Short Bio

LyndaU 'the brand', is an experienced Business Development professional. Beyond the corporate milieu, she mentors at Durham University, volunteers with the Special Marshal arm of the Federal Road Safety Corps in Nigeria, and at various orphanages.

She loves children and has adopted a number of orphanages and supports them through her young NGO 'Our Old Become their New', which she uses as her vehicle to collect books and toys. She believes every child should be exposed to these so as to preserve their fun childhood. Artist. Model. Ardent sports lover. She can be contacted at 3sistersintl@gmail.com or on LinkedIn: Lynda Umeh MBA

Madhuri Tirumandas, MD

Life on the NJ Turnpike
Madhuri Tirumandas

IND

Landing in Newark International Airport, we took the ride on the turnpike. My dad asked *"How do you like America?"* It's not home, is all I knew. I felt so small in a huge world with nothing to call home. Not like India where I had lived with my grandparents.

It wasn't really my choice to move to a brand new country. I have done it before. We lived in New Zealand briefly and I disliked it as a child. This was somehow supposed to be better? I wasn't too sure about that as a skinny, dark-skinned, ambitious little girl who was always polite and nice to others.

My journey began in New Jersey high school. I was very alone for most of 9th grade. I didn't like lunch because I couldn't afford it and my mom packed the most boring lunches of all. Break times were lonely. At least in class people copied my math homework, or I was part of some group project. These kids were my

friends right? Nope. I realized soon that there were others like me and all of us formed a group. We found some hope in the hopeless high school hallways.

I got into college and our close-knit group had to split up. My parents wanted me to choose medicine or engineering. I had to choose quickly because they couldn't afford to pay for my medical degree in America and it was shorter to do it in India. I thought about my grandfather, who really wanted me to become a doctor because he believed there's no other profession like it. I have always been passionate about helping others. Maybe medicine is the way to go?

I started college two exits north of where we lived off the NJ turnpike and commuted daily. I picked a major that would get me the most approval - Biomedical Engineering. I wanted approval in every way. College finally allowed me to be myself, and engage in simple activities like getting my eyebrows done. I could afford to go on a trip as a teenager and live without my parents, and without their permission. My grandparents had allowed me to do so much back in India. But I couldn't even step into a different part of my parents' house to randomly paint, draw, or talk to a friend on the phone without their approval.

I felt very controlled.

One way I could get my power back was to do everything I could to get approval from my parents. I did well in school, I didn't drink alcohol. I wanted close friends, so I stuck to the two close friends I made in high school. My parents also approved of them so anything I did with them received a green light. Bingo! I found my small freedoms of drives away from home, trips to stay over with both of them at their different colleges.

I became an emergency medical technician (EMT) to start exploring my interest in medicine and my passion grew stronger with each patient on the ambulance. I embraced Engineers Without Borders, helping a community in Guatemala with their water supply project as an undergraduate empowered me as a human. I found friends through this organization who were just as passionate to help others as I was.

Finally, I started feeling like my own person again.

After completing medical school in the Caribbean and matching into internal medicine residency, I felt invincible. I had finally arrived! That was until I was smacked in the face by anxiety and depression! All of which likely stemmed from the approval-seeking over years and years, my own perfectionism and highest of standards I had set for myself.

This was not the time to be shy.

My immigrant parents and family didn't recognize mental health as a diagnosis. It was just improper thought that we can snap out of. But I leveraged being a physician-in-training, and I knew I needed help. I pushed through, got professional help, and accepted that the journey I had-had thus so far was a survival mechanism.

I had to stop fighting who I was and stop the need-for-approval cycle.

My medical residency finished and I finally decided to practice not just with purpose in life but to act out of my own true values. I began to respect my growth. I started setting my own values and standards in life. Mistakes are ok, they are an opportunity to grow. I was enough. I am enough... Everyday I just had to be a little better than the day before.

I was fine.

I am fine the way God created me. And that's what

truly empowers me every single day to be the best Infectious Diseases physician I can be through the COVID pandemic.

My Proudest Accomplishment

I think one of my biggest accomplishments in life is overcoming depression and anxiety while being a brand new medical resident.

Residency in itself carries its new challenges. But reaching out for help, accepting that anxiety and depression were a problem for me, will always be my proudest moment. Most immigrant parents and families are not in tune with mental health. They don't consider it a true illness. However for me, it was the biggest accomplishment of my entire life.

The greatest breakthrough for me was; acknowledging my own mental health battles as I supported my patients through their most vulnerable times. To this date, my parents do not even approve of speaking about this, however, I realize that is part of my immigrant journey. And I want to truly empower humans around me every day to recognize their mental illness, support them and encourage them to seek help.

Biggest Life Lesson

I don't think I've ever been as exhausted as I am

currently, being a COVID doctor. I experienced depression and anxiety through residency. Out of that came a lot of mental health support work I started myself. I started a wellness program in my residency, I trained in SMART-R (Stress Management and Resiliency Training - for Residents) and trained my fellows during my infectious disease fellowship.

However, seeing the number of deaths, the hopelessness that COVID has carried the entire healthcare system through, is mentally, physically and emotion-

...and find balance in connecting with my fellow healthcare warriors...

ally exhausting. It has created an inner turmoil which I have battled through 2020 and beyond. Moreover, the entire world asking me questions and looking for answers and believing people who are not physicians, or specialists in the fields of infectious diseases, immunology or critical care pushes me deeper and deeper into pain and exhaustion.

The only coping mechanism I've found right now that works is to ignore it completely. Block out all the news. Block out the opinions of others. This is to truly focus on my patients who are on ventilators and requiring maximum support, the patients who are in the same room as their spouse struggling to breathe, and the nurses and respiratory therapists tirelessly working with each patient in protective gear and struggling to comfortably breathe under N95 masks.

When questions pop up such as *"Do you think I should clean my vegetables with this dish soap or that dish soap?"* or *"I really want to attend this gathering, do you think it's a good idea?"*, or *"Have you heard of this new treatment? It seems to be the cure for COVID. I read it on our group WhatsApp message"*, I'm no longer just angry and frustrated. I'm simply numb.

I exit the conversation physically and mentally, and find balance in connecting with my fellow healthcare warriors battling this on the frontlines on a daily basis. I've found peace in my meditation practice and started a short practice of yoga.

Journaling these feelings and having regular counseling sessions is helping my soul stay on the bright side and not take a dark turn.

On Staying Mentally Stable...

I always remind myself: *"Every adversity, every failure, every heartbreak, carries with it the seed of an equal or greater benefit"*
– Napoleon Hill.

What does that mean? Adversity doesn't sound good at all you might say. But if I wasn't that 9th grader who moved to America, I wouldn't have had the opportunity to be immersed in the American culture and the opportunities that I have today. I wouldn't have been open to new cultures. I wouldn't have embraced all the friends of different backgrounds who are part of my life now.

When I came across any immigrant patient in my residency and fellowship training, I connected the most with them. I spoke their language, I felt their pain, I felt the uncertainty they had in their eyes. I held their to calm them down because I was prescribing a new medication, and I earned their trust instantly. And that was all because of the adversity I went through as a teenager.

We understood and vibed with our common adversities. I felt a sense of purpose from all of my adversity. I benefited from everyone's heart I touched and every illness I was part of to help improve and eventually cure.

To empathize and aid another man or woman's pain at vulnerable times in their lives was no longer an adversity, but a gift that God gave me to give to others and impact their lives. I believe it is my destiny and my life's work to fulfill it.

Two favorite quotes

"You see, some things I can teach you. Some you learn from books. But there are things that, well, you have to see and feel."
– Khaled Hosseini from *A Thousand Splendid Suns*

"Always do the right thing, not because you may gain something by it, but because it is right"
– My elementary school English

Dream legacy

I'd like to leave behind an organization that continues to help underserved areas of the world with food, health care and basic necessities of life. This is in the works!

How I center myself

Throughout my journey into immigration and into assimilation of American culture, I had to find ways that made me and my soul relax and rest. One way is to speak to my family. I am rooted in my grandparents' mission to help and impact as many lives as possible in every way that I am able to.

Volunteering at the library, hospital, at a hospice, on the ambulance as an EMT, all gave me a sense of calm, somehow relaxed my soul and gave me a sense of purpose. I also love to meditate, listen to music, put on a candle and read a personal development book, knowing that it can help me become a better version of myself. Hiking up mountains lifts my soul up at my lowest points. Nature is one of my best therapies. And a warm, delicious meal never fails to bring me pure joy.

Little Madhuri's dream

When I was really young, a common question I was asked was *"What do you want to be when you grow up - a doctor like all your aunts or an engineer like your dad?"* I didn't know for the most part but I felt a passion towards helping others.

I did that throughout college, being part of Engineers Without Borders, as part of an emergency rescue squad, while volunteering, and everyday as an infectious diseases physician battling the COVID pandemic. Moving here didn't change my passion, in fact my passion to help others kept me grounded throughout my journey of adjusting to a whole new culture.

For the next generation

Do not give up on your passion and dreams. Life gets in the way. I get it. But life isn't supposed to be fun, easy and chill all the time. In fact, you grow the most at the lowest points in life. We're all born for a purpose. Connect with it, connect with your inner power, because in the lowest points in life, that's what will carry you through. And you can then truly be empowered, and thus empower everyone around you.

Thankful

I'm most thankful for my grandfather... He's the one who helped me create the vision and legacy I mentioned above.

I thank him and my grandmother for their audacity to move from a small village to a city, start a whole new life, and set the stage to help his kids and grandkids immigrate to America to give us the best possible future. I will forever be grateful for them and the lessons they taught me.

Short Bio

Madhuri Tirumandas is a board certified Infectious Diseases physician practicing in New Jersey. She practices mindfulness regularly and prioritizes health & wellness to be the best physician she can be. Outside of medicine, she strives to add value to the community around her and uplift all humans she comes in contact with. She believes in truly living out of purpose, values and passions in life no matter what.

Fire Unextinguished

Maneesha Ahluwalia

IND

That afternoon you were so angry in your own home that you flipped over the entire dining room table for all to see. The room was shocked. They knew you had anger. They did not know you had rage. You did not mean to scare them. You did not mean to create fear in them.

In apology, to avoid being the cause of their shock, to be the girl you were supposed to be, to receive the praise you had seen being offered to Payal who was not even your family, to get out of the feeling that was stuck in the pit of your chest, bubbling up to the surface in words but never coming out, you kept a distance from you, you quieted your own self, you silenced the one wanting to be heard, kicking, screaming, fighting, rebelling, loving, hating, wanting. I know what you wanted. You did not. How could you? You were nine years old.

That human did a bad thing. It was wrong. He did it anyway. He walked away. He left you with feelings too complicated for a nine-year-old girl to understand. You raged, kicked, screamed, rebelled, loved, hated, wanted. Isn't that what happened? Did that even happen? When you think back on that day that he did that to you, you remember, don't you? I know you remember each detail.

You remember the darkness of the room, the silky sheets on the bed, the writing on the pillow covers, the voices of other grown-ups and Payal in the other room, the commands he gave, the features of his face, the mustache, the glasses, and now as you think of him, you have disgust. You were only nine. How could you have known it was wrong, because somehow the feelings you had were right, and the feelings you had were wrong. Could it have been that it was

wrong and it felt good? But then was THAT wrong? To feel good from something like that?

I know what you wanted. You did not. How could you? This was the first time you felt that way.

Your womanhood started at age nine. You were in the fourth grade, in the classroom, and your womanhood left a red spot on your classroom chair, and because the teacher told you to tie that shirt around your waist, you did.

You hid the truth so others would not be uncomfortable, so they would not have to see. You were told by them to stay silent unless you could talk like Payal. You were told by them that it is best to hide and not speak of your truths.

If this, then praise. If this, then good. If this, then you are allowed. You were given permission to be you, within limits. Those were the rules. There it began. The fire. Rage, kicking, screaming, fighting, rebelling, hating, loving, wanting.

My dear. My sweetheart. My baby. You have known. You have carried a fire. You have been willing to be with your fire just long enough, just enough to feel the heat in your eyes, just go close enough to have the tips of your fingers go numb from the heat, just enough so you could feel the warm praise of the fire, and then, be on the hunt for that which could

extinguish that fire, that could wipe out the hope, the goodness, the love.

To that I answer…

I know now. I didn't know then.

I met a boy, and I agreed to marry that boy, and it just wasn't right for me. I met the next one, and he was perfect. However, my parents who had given me everything did not approve of him. My Indian parents were unable to accept my Nigerian boyfriend, not then. I left him. I felt relief. I felt anguish. The sweet, innocent, oh! Such glorious love of a man who was so full of love. I grieved the loss of that love for years, wandering crowded-but-empty-for-me streets of New York City.

I was asked to leave my very first job as a physician. They told me I was not enough. I did not bring enough money for the business. Business? I thought I was a physician, helping patients, at a hospital. My heart pounds even now as I think back to that moment of being told of my inadequacy. I believed them and I left. I grieved the loss of "enoughness" that I had built up. Fire. Rage. Kicking. Screaming. Wanting.

I went to volunteer in Kenya. I breathed life into my soul again. Passion for patients, love for a man, and zest for life was back. The mission came to an end. I was prepared to stay for him. He said I was not

enough. I did not stay home enough, cook enough, refrain from socializing enough. He left. I grieved in excruciating pain. Fire. Rage. Kicking. Screaming. Fighting. Rebelling. Loving. Hating. Wanting.

Why wasn't anyone seeing me!?

I met a fellow humanitarian. We met. We fell in love hard and fast. He was perfect and said he shared my dreams to volunteer in the world. We agreed to spend our lives doing just that. He joined me in my volunteer journey. We returned from our adventure. He changed his tune. He changed.

He wanted me to have his children. He wanted me and us to stop our volunteer journey. He wanted a home and a stable life with children. I wanted the life I wanted when we had met years prior. Three long years we spent here, wanting different lives. He gave me a final thirty days, and I continued to fight until he couldn't wait any longer. He left.

This pain. It was a lack of feeling. A stillness. A numbness. A lack of feeling!!! The worst kind of feeling for a feeling-seeker who was used to feeling. Fire. Rage. Kicking. Screaming. Fighting. Rebelling.

Loving. Hating. Wanting. Stillness. The stillness was worse than any pain I had ever felt. There was no peace in that stillness. There was no calm. It was an unrelenting discomfort. The stillness was begging me to hear my own voice and exercise my choice. "What choice?" I asked myself. There was no choice here. Who was I to have a choice and voice?

I gave in. I promised to try. We tried for three years to have children. In those three years, while trying, I started to hear new thoughts. As I started to hear new thoughts, I started to believe new thoughts. My Indian upbringing had not come with these thoughts. I was never exposed to these thoughts. No, never. I was in a community of mostly white women. They spoke in their voices as if they had choices in their lives.

Wait. Wait one second. Choice is an option? The choice is mine? I have a choice? I have a voice? What voice? I had never heard my own voice until now. Forty-four years old. I began to hear MY voice.

My baby, I hear you. You wanted me to hear you all those years. Through Fire. Rage. Kicking. Screaming. Fighting. Rebelling. Loving. Hating. You wanted my love for you. Of course you wanted my love for you. Of course you did, my love. You were denied all the love that was right here, within. I had it this entire time. I had so much love. I gave and gave, yet received only

inadequacy back. I had a choice now to receive love from none other than myself? Was it truly possible? OH YES!

My sweetheart, my love, my baby. I love you. Right now. I love you. I love you first. You have been a human, a human with human thoughts, feelings; and you have taken actions, and I never spoke with you, only judged you. I never loved you, only loathed you. So now, when there are no children then he says I don't satisfy him enough. Yes. Again. I hear I'm not enough. This time. No. It's me I hear. I hear me. I hear you, loud and clear. I fight for you, and I fight for us. You first. Us first. Me first.

This we never learned, did we? Except you knew all along. You wanted me to fight for you first, for us first, for me first? You knew that's what you wanted. I give love freely now. To you. You are me. I am you. You and I have a voice. We have a choice. And we have love. Big, unbounding, unchained, unconditional love.

Let him say I am not enough for him. Channel that unconditional love for us, and let it flow to him. He is wanting just like you were. You gave me permission to stay on our journey. You knew what was best for you and for me this entire time. You knew what you wanted. Does it even matter what they said or did or wanted? Now that I know that we can speak our true language of love, big, expansive love, a language only we understand, now that that is realized, there is nothing else.

Let others come to experience it from us, with us. Let us share it. We have it and now let's give it. Radically. There are Indians. There are Indian girls. There are little Indian girls growing up to be Indian women. What if they haven't found choice, voice, or

What if the new dream is just this?
What if this isn't new?

unconditional love for themselves, and what if that is all they've ever wanted, from themselves? Let's attract them. You and me. Let's bring them in. Let's love them until they find the love they have for themselves.

What if the new dream is just this? What if this isn't new? What if this was always the plan? What if this is exactly how the life you have lived was supposed to be? Fire. Rage. Kicking. Screaming. Fighting. Rebelling. Loving. Hating. Wanting. It was all ok. It was always ok. It was the fuel. It IS you, me, and us. It is part of us. It stays with us for a reason. Fire leads us, helps us, holds us.

I know now, and I'm just catching up to you. You, little girl, you always knew.

You have always had love in abundance. Fire, unextinguished.

Is there anything else you want the world to know about you?
What I want the world to know is that unconditional love lies within you, waiting to be realized. Your community, your family, your soul, they will receive it only after you hold it, keep it. As such, you become part of the human connection, the human force of loving energy that unites us, heals us, brings us energy to truly live.

What is one thing you are most proud of as an immigrant?
As a child of immigrants, we first generationers prosper because our parents came to America. They did, therefore we are. I'm most proud that we live in harmony in this in-between world.

What would you never leave your home without?
I would never leave my house without my smile. My smile creates joy and radiates warmth into my surroundings, for others to feel, for others to hold.

What do you do to relax, unwind and refill your cup?
I refill my cup through tears rolling down my face, doubled over holding my stomach, uncontrollable belly laughs.

My mom, my brother, my cousin, and a dear friend – they all share these belly laughs with me. The urge for rolling laughter arises. We succumb. Afterwards: amazing contentment. So, I laugh! Belly laughs.

As a child, what did you want to be when you grew up?
My dream was to perform on stage when I grew up. Coaching, playing tennis, engaging in partnerships with others, each one of these experiences is a performance on stages, redefined. My immigrant background is what adds depth to each of these parts of my whole.

Short bio
Dr. Maneesha Ahluwalia is an American-born Indian woman. She is a Life Coach and an Infectious Disease Physician. As a Life Coach, Dr. Ahluwalia works with Indian professionals ready to feel proud of their choices and have love for their parents so they can create the connection they crave. She is a #warriorwoman and a #surthrivor. Dr. Ahluwalia can be reached at drmaneeshaahluwalia@gmail.com.

Ready to Love Again!

Martha Ebele Schmidt

NGA / USA

England! Where it All Started

Growing up in England as a little girl, I attended Gwyn Jones Primary School on Hainault road in East London. I remember we walked to school during the summer in those days, on the way back we played hopscotch sometimes. Home wasn't far and it was always fun having a bunch of other kids to walk home with as we laughed and talked; just happy being kids. I enjoyed growing up in London, I liked my school, my friends and I remember "Mr. Curry".

Mr. Curry was the school headmaster, but more importantly he was the teacher who helped me discover, through gymnastics, the power of my own body. I loved the way I could twist and move my body, climb the ropes, use the trapeze, handstand and cartwheel all in one performance. He believed in me, saw my potential and encouraged me.

My parents left London and moved back to Nigeria after their residency ended. Before the United Kingdom, we moved from the United States of America where we had also lived for five years. I attended Booker T. Washington elementary school in Kentucky. I don't recall if there were any white kids in that school but I do remember almost everyone was black.

Moving back home to Nigeria at the tender age of 12 was a huge culture shock for me in so many ways. Things, people, and places were so different. I learnt to adjust and found myself settling in quickly to a new way of life.

A very shy, young girl growing up in a very religious home, I didn't speak much. We were always told to hush as children and so I grew up thinking my opinion never really mattered. It was always the other person's desire over mine and eventually I got used to living that way. My desire to please seemed pretty normal to me.

Ghana, First Go!

It was no wonder therefore, when "Terfa" showed up in my life, that all I wanted to do was to help him get his own life back even if this was to my detriment. I didn't care, I was on a mission I believed, a good one. I remember the attraction for me then was to help him get his failing life back together - he was a drug addict... but I loved him. I saw his soul and the person he was really trying to be, a good man. I decided to give him a chance, a chance with my life, and we got married.

We had a son soon enough but Terfa never recovered from his addiction, instead it got worse. I thought maybe if we relocated to another country he would leave the old lifestyle behind and be more willing to embrace the new. And so in the spirit of the people-pleaser that I was, I gave up my wonderful, thriving career as an ace broadcaster at one of the top radio stations in the city of Lagos, Nigeria, along with the perks that came with it, and moved.

We moved to Ghana.

The Gold Coast as it is fondly called was a wonderful experience for me. The people of Ghana are very warm and friendly people. Akwaaba! Like Nigerians, they are also very colorful when adorned in their national Kente attire. I was blessed with 2 more children while in Ghana for the almost 5 years I was there with Terfa. I met amazing people from all over the world, some of whom have become lifelong friends, but most of all I grew while in Ghana.

As a result of my growth, I was able to see that there was more to me than my marriage. Unbeknownst to me, my desire to return to Nigeria would eventually lead to my separation. He had become violent by the day, spiralling out of control like a man losing the war with himself slowly, but surely.

Moving back to Nigeria, I became stronger inside of myself, my mind clearer and my heart calmer. With a strength of might I didn't know I possessed, I made the big decision to leave. Big because this was not the norm in Nigeria then, I knew it wasn't going to be easy. The laws that govern the land do not generally favor women. In Nigeria, a woman didn't just get to leave her husband's home, and definitely NOT with the kids.

Many times I really believed Terfa was under some kind of spell he just couldn't break free from. He was a good man with a kind heart, but for some unknown reason, he could not move past this wall in his life. The

drugs controlled him and seemed to be all he lived for. When we returned to Nigeria, he became more violent, more aggressive, more desperate. Things became so hard for me and the kids.

Our lives and livelihood had fallen apart. I hadn't been able to get work since we returned, and as I was the breadwinner, our savings hemorrhaged. I remember the last time I went to the bank just to find out he had withdrawn all the money we had, every single dime, gone! I was horrified and so hurt. I stood there looking at the teller in shock, completely speechless.

The kids were thrown out of school after that. I was drowning and couldn't find my way up.

I prayed. I fasted. I cried. I hoped.

I waited patiently for a miracle, until it was clear to me, that the only miracle coming was me running away with the kids. I had seen this in movies but actually coming up with a plot to escape in real life was nothing I had imagined for myself, yet this seemed the only way out, and so it was set in motion.

One early Sunday morning in January 2013, as he was lying on the couch in the living room, I had gotten the kids up earlier and had dressed them up. When he asked where we were going, I replied quietly and said we were going to church. I was afraid to say anything that would set him off.

Unknown to him, the night before I had sent a suitcase filled with my things and the kids' things over to a friend's house. I didn't know what I was doing but I knew I couldn't take any more abuse from a mentally unstable man. It was a risk but I was ready to take it, so out the door we went, never to return.

Ghana, Again!

I escaped to Ghana, second time around with my son and 2 daughters to get away from everything - the abuse, the hurt, the shame, the neglect. Yes, this time my move was for me and, of course, my kids. We needed a break, a change in pace and an opportunity to heal. My back and forth love affair with Ghana was a reality, and I remain ever grateful to the country and people of Ghana for giving me somewhere else to call home when I needed one.

When Terfa died I cried hard. I still remember it vividly. I received a message from his brother via Facebook that he had passed on and the burial was in about 2 weeks. It was an emotional time for me and the kids.

I didn't attend the funeral.

In Nigeria the law does not favor women. I didn't want to risk losing my children, nor be accused of killing someone I hadn't seen in a whole year. If I had attempted to return at that time for the funeral, that would have been my plight, so I stayed back.

Looking back at my life, I have done some tremendous work on myself. My guiding principles today are self-love and self-worth. Learning through my pain and struggle, it took a while to accept myself as strong and beautiful. I have however, learned to love and pay attention to myself. I now focus more on my strengths and don't worry too much about any weaknesses, as I give more attention to the former, the latter fades.

And then came Gene.....

I eventually moved back to Nigeria the following year, when I felt the coast was clear. I was happy to be offered a job at my former place of employment, but this time as head of 3 major radio stations in Abuja. I loved my job, it exposed me to influencers; wining and dining with heads of states, ambassadors, celebrities and the likes, walking in the corridors of power, until I met Gene...

...the man in my dreams, the one I danced with late into the night, went on walks with by the beach, flew to Hawaii with, all in my romantic head.

It wasn't until four years later, when I was visiting the US for a Bob Proctor conference that Gene and I met on a blind date set up by my sister. From "Hello", our souls seemed to merge, like I knew this stranger from another dimension. Gene was the man in my dreams, it was easy to be with him. He was selfless and caring, it felt like his dream was to make my dreams come true!

Love is all around us and waiting for us whenever we are ready.

From Lagos to New York to Abuja to California, ours was a whirlwind romance. We held hands in the sun, drove up the mountains, cruised on the ocean and cried in the rain, the signs were everywhere! The universe was actively nudging us on from the first date we had in the US, to the many others that followed on the West coast of Africa. From the instant joy we both felt when we first met, to the tears we both shed when it was time for me to leave. Things were happening so fast but I was ready for this moment, ready to love again!

The first time Gene told me he wanted to come to Nigeria I really thought he was joking and laughed it off. However, this had become a burning desire within him. It was no surprise when he eventually received his visa after an initial delay, got his malaria shots, booked his flight and was airborne, bound for Africa for the very first time! It was on the shores of Africa, in the city of Lagos that I fell in love with this beautiful soul.

Love is all around us and waiting for us whenever we are ready. It is never too late to love, and so at the age of 48, I became a bride again. With one knee bent and a beautiful diamond ring, Gene asked me to be his wife in sunny California. We did fly to Hawaii, this time not in my dreams but on our honeymoon where I fell in love all over again. Aloha!

As with any change comes new challenges and I have had my fair share. Getting my 3 children to join me in the US has been the first of many. Living with an adult step son with a traumatic brain injury has also been a learning curve for me. I have learnt patience in new ways.

How do you face challenges mentally?

I find that in times of great pressure to quit, or back out of something, repeating powerful affirmations relevant to the situation help me stay sane. Saying the words with feelings help realign my mind to my goal.

Lunch with?

Oprah and invite her to visit Nigeria, the most populous Black nation in the world. I've always felt you haven't visited Africa until you've visited Nigeria. Did you know that one out of every five persons of African origin is a Nigerian?

Favorite quote

"Our deepest fear is not that we are inadequate. Our deepest fear is that we are powerful beyond measure..."
– Marianne Williamson

How do you relax?

I always love a good read, listening to music and inspirational audios get my juices going. I find writing to be cathartic.

Thanks...

To my late father always for the discipline he instilled in me. A kind gentleman who taught me the importance of integrity and honesty as a child. These tenets have molded me into the woman I am today.

Short Bio

Martha is a Marketing Consultant, Broadcaster and an Inspirational Speaker. A wife and mother of 4. She lives in Southern California where the sun shines all year round! Martha is passionate about empowering women and young girls. Through her annual women's conference "Cinderella, There's Greatness in You!", Martha speaks to inspire women from all walks of life. As a survivor of domestic abuse, Martha shares her story, and offers counseling to hurting women. Reach Martha at marthasfables2@gmail.com

Senses of My Childhood

Mia Yang

CHN / USA

Sound

Crack! Crack! Crack! I sat on the concrete steps of our local park with my grandfather, listening to kids playing whipping top on the concrete floor. I hugged my knees, trying to express to YieYie that I felt out of place back in China. At 19 years old, I spent the past seven years focused on only one thing, assimilating myself into American society. I pushed those pains of being separate from grandparents and my aunt deep within. It was too painful to sit with the discomfort that my childhood family will always be separated from my parents and my life in America. Crack! The whip spun the wooden tops hypnotically.

After meeting up with my elementary school best friends for lunch, we could not find common topics to talk about. They joked that my handwriting had become messier when I used to have the best hand-writing among all of us. I asked about their college lives knowing that my life had already diverged dramatically from theirs. YieYie had been so proud when he heard about me getting a merit scholarship for college. Ming could not afford college and YieYie gave her money to contribute to an associate's degree. He told Ming that it was from me and my parents. I had no idea until he told me recently.

"Don't forget your Chinese," YieYie said. *"We have over two thousand years of history and culture. Now you'll always have that with you."*

Touch

I felt his rough hands and saw the old age spots on my patient's hand as I tried to find the best place to draw blood. His hand looked like YieYie's hand, long fingers, speckled, dignified. I refocused my attention to hear him call out to his wife, bragging to her about me as his "Greek granddaughter." They had no idea that I had a panic attack outside their home thirty minutes earlier. As a second year internal medicine resident at Johns Hopkins Bayview Medical Center, I had a panel of homebound older adults in the community surrounding the hospital to be their primary care doctor.

Mr. G had dementia and lived downstairs in the basement of a typical Baltimore row home. He could no longer climb the stairs to go upstairs and had to be carried out of the house by ambulance every time he left his home for a doctor's appointment. Thirty minutes ago I was overwhelmed with tears, not sure why I suddenly could not go into my patient's home for a scheduled home visit. I sat in my car, trying to take deep breaths. I called the Elder House Call office, hoping to reschedule, but Mary must've stepped out of the office as I only reached her voicemail. I tried calling Alex, my fiancé at the time, but he did not answer as he was working as a Hospitalist. Out of options and feeling the obligation, I pulled myself together and dried my tears as best as I could.

It was not until sitting in the Student Health therapist's chair later in the year did I make the connection between YieYie's death the year before and my panic attack before my house calls that day. I loved the intimacy of seeing patients in their own homes. I loved the humanity of it all. But I could not get past the severe anxiety it provoked. I had second thoughts about getting a fellowship in geriatrics then, with the application/match process inching closer. Was this really what I wanted to do with my life in medicine? Become a geriatrician who has panic attacks treating older adults?

I pushed those pains...deep within.

Sometimes our greatest fears are also our greatest loves. In this case I did get past my fear and panic by age 27. House calls really made me fall in love with geriatrics. I decided to stay at Johns Hopkins for a geriatric fellowship and looked for a job that would allow me to lead a house call program. Today, I am proud to say that I am in charge of a team that provides home-based medical care to close to two hundred patients in North Carolina.

Smell

My mom sprinkled some dried chili powder on the potato pancakes and immediately it reminded me

of the street food of my youth. It smelled vaguely of nuts, chili, and a tinge of nostalgia. I used to love to eat potato patties grilled on a small portable grill outside of my elementary school. Street vendors would have small plastic chairs in front of their grill and holler at passersby for business. You could put all kinds of spices and nuts mixed with the scallion potato pancakes cooked to order. I used to buy them with allowance money on my way home from school.

My hometown's biggest export is chili oil. We can now find them in Asian grocery stores. Rice wine, chili, and unpolluted air are reasons why people from big cities like BeiJing and ShangHai visit our province. I still remember a stranger commenting at the airport that GuiZhou people were country, *"backward"*, uneducated folks, completely oblivious to the fact that someone like me was sitting beside them biting my tongue about being born and raised there.

My son's head smells like baby skin, shampoo, and innocence. He, along with his older sister has never been to China. I worry about how they'll adapt there, with everything being so crowded and loud. My daughter dislikes dirt and will turn her nose at my parents' Chinese cooking. My son is finally at a picky toddler stage and will shake his head and spit out the peas and edamame that are mixed in with fried rice.

Their childhoods are so drastically different from mine, I am both excited and nervous that they will feel out of place in their mixed Chinese-Jewish heritage, never truly belonging in either group. It has only been a recent development in my life that I tell myself to choose "AND" rather than "OR". I am not Chinese or American, I am both. I spent years feeling like I don't belong anywhere as an immigrant but the more I read about other immigrants' stories, the more I am convinced that the *"OR"* narrative in my mind does not serve me. My life is more expansive and interesting because of *"AND"* and I intend to pass on the joy of the duality to my children.

Sight

I do not have any pictures from the one time I saw my mother during our nine years apart. She had come to drop off my infant brother when he was seven months old back in China. I remember my mother and my brother's visit with trepidation, suddenly I was a big sister in a nation of only children.

As an eight-year-old, my memories of my mother were so fuzzy that I could not distinguish what was truly my own memory and what were the stories that I was told. I have a mental picture of myself sleeping in bed with my mom and my brother the first night they

came home to GuiYang. I was curled up on the opposite side of the bed, staring at my mother's arched feet. I never saw my father once during the ten years that we were apart.

When I came to the US at age twelve, I did not speak any English and no family members could travel with me. So my grandfather made me a cardboard sign that I wore around my neck that stated my name in Chinese and in English, address, and contact information for my parents. Upon arrival at Newark NJ airport, I looked for my father among the crowds. A man around 50 years old or so came up to me and introduced himself as my father. He smiled and looked at me tentatively. But somehow he did not look like the picture of my father that my grandfather had shown me. *"You're not my BaBa"*, I told him, puzzled. He broke into a mischievous laugh and then my real father came out from somewhere behind him. Turns out my maternal uncle wanted to play this joke on me just to test whether I could be accidentally lured away by a stranger.

Taste

My parents brought moon cake and almond cookies during their last visit. My children devoured the almond cookies but refused to eat the perfect egg yolk inside the moon cake. A moon cake is a classic Chinese dessert shared during Mid-Autumn Festival, where an egg yolk is encased within not-too-sweet red bean paste and covered with dough. I remember the irony of the Mid-Autumn Festival when I first arrived in the US in Sept 1997, a time when families are supposed to be getting together, I was flying from one end of the world to the other.

I sat on the front porch watching my father playing peekaboo with my son, making him giggle, holding

Sometimes our greatest fears are also our greatest loves.

his hands so that my son could take his first steps. My mother was reading a book with my daughter on her lap, trying to hold her left hand steady so that it does not accidentally shake too much from her Parkinson's disease.

My parents brought all of my favorite homemade dishes, taking my requests, shopping, and cooking over multiple days. They mixed their love within sweet and spicy short ribs and twice cooked pork. They made sure to cook dishes without any spicy ingredients for my children and joyously fed them bites at the dining room table. *"Have you eaten yet?"* Or *"What have you eaten?"* are the love greetings of millions of Asian parents. My mother often laments wistfully that if we lived in the same city as them, we could come over any time for dinner. Instead, more and more I find myself interested in recreating their recipes, stocking up on Pi Jian Dou Ban and "Old Grandma" chili at Asian grocery stores.

What one lesson has life taught you that you would like to share to inspire the next generation?
Out of our greatest challenges, we learn the most. Whenever life is hard, just remember that everything is temporary and one day you will look back and realize how much you've grown.

What do you do to relax, unwind and refill your cup?
I enjoy reading, catching up on fun shows on Netflix, and spending time with my family. I am also trying to be more consistent with meditation and exercise. I am a daily journal writer and always write about what I am grateful for, send out good thoughts into the universe, and write self-affirmations.

What one thing are you most proud of as an immigrant?
I am very proud of my discipline/work ethic and

my ability to empathize with people from all backgrounds. I understand how it feels to be an outsider and I am curious about everyone's stories. I am also proud of the Chinese value of honoring and respecting our elders. I chose to be a geriatrician because I love older adults.

What legacy would you leave behind?

Professionally, I would like to make meaningful changes that translate research innovations into daily lives of older adults living with dementia and ways to better support family caregivers.

Personally, I hope to raise compassionate and socially-active children who believe in their own power. I hope to make people smile when they think of memories of me.

As a child, what did you want to be when you grew up? Are you doing that now? Did emigrating change or affect that in any way?

As a child, I wanted to be a scientist. I loved reading biographies/short-stories of famous scientists around the world. I am a physician researcher now. Although I do not work in a lab with test tubes, I am using the scientific method to test ways of improving our broken American healthcare system to better care for older adults, especially those living with dementia, and better support their family caregivers.

Short Bio

Mia Yang, MD MS is a Chinese-American physician-researcher who is passionate about improving healthcare for vulnerable older adults in the community. She is the Director for Wake Forest House Call Program which cares for homebound patients with home-based medical care. She is an investigator within the Wake Forest Alzheimer's Disease Research Center, funded by the National Institute of Health. She lives in Winston-Salem, North Carolina with her husband, a Palliative Medicine Doctor/former Hospitalist, and two children. In her spare time, she enjoys reading, making crafts with her kids, and cooking French toast and bacon on the weekends.

The Emergence
Obiageli Ogbata

NGA / USA

Childhood Dreams

I was one child who liked to get her vaccinations because it meant that I got to see my pediatrician. She was a very pretty woman and was always well dressed. I wanted to grow up to be like her - a doctor.

Upon graduating high school, I gained admission to a medical school in eastern Nigeria to study medicine and surgery. The years flew by very quickly, before long, I was graduating from medical school. It was during my internship year that I was introduced to my would-be husband.

He came to Nigeria to visit and we decided to take the bold step and get married. Our getting married meant I had to move to the United States; change my name, my abode; leave my family and friends; and embrace a whole new culture. And that began my new life; a new family.

America - Adventure Into the Future

We landed at JFK International Airport in mid January 2005. We arrived in Charlotte, North Carolina (NC) a few days later. The week after we got to Charlotte, he started his new job. I was home alone, 6000 miles from home. That was when the biggest challenges began, there was a sickening quietness that filled the house when he was at work. This was before the era of smartphones, facetime and social media. Next on my to-do list was to get my medical licensing exams out of the way and apply for residency in internal medicine. This process started just before Kathryn, my first child was born.

I elected to sign for an internal medicine residency position with Newark Beth Israel Medical Center (NBIMC) outside of the residency match program. A few weeks later, I had my second child, Kenny. I was elated to be a wife, mother and soon-to-be resident.

Tough Choices

As the start date for residency drew closer, it became evident to me that I was going to be moving to New Jersey alone with my very young children. Their father planned to visit on the weekends or when he was not working. This arrangement was not very palatable at the time but it appeared that there was nothing that could be done about it.

Regardless, I thoroughly enjoyed residency. I enjoyed internal medicine in medical school, and was glad that I had chosen it as a career path. In the first few months of training, I developed a love for oncology. I had also come to really enjoy pulmonary/critical care. The intensive care unit was the perfect sanctuary for me with my "fixer personality".

I had the opportunity to make changes and immediately see the impact the changes made in often critically ill people. However, after the fellowship applications opened up in my 2nd year of residency training, I applied for hematology/oncology (hem/onc) fellowship. There were three other applicants from my class alone. I felt that I had a good chance - I was smart, hardworking and was a team player. But that also described the other 3 applicants. Well, match day came and I did not match into the fellowship program.

First, I was disappointed, then a little angry but these feelings were soon replaced by feelings of rejection and the awkwardness that I felt showing up to work the next few days. The easier route may have been to be angry, show resentment and be bitter, after all, no one enjoys being rejected. But, I chose to be mature, keep a bold face, continue to work diligently and accept the fellowship outcome in good faith.

That experience has turned out to be one of my biggest character building opportunities. Through it all, I learned that a closed door is oftentimes access to open windows and even bigger opportunities.

> *I felt that I had a good chance - I was smart, hardworking and was a team player.*

One year flew by and it was another application season. By this time, I was really excelling in the Intensive Care Unit (ICU) so much so that the ICU director offered me a pulmonary/critical (pulm/crit) care fellowship outside of the match. This was very complimentary because we had 7 internal candidates in addition to innumerable external candidates competing for 3 pulm/crit care positions. My colleagues

thought I was crazy to not take the pre-match offer. That was a tough decision to make but I followed my heart and decided to go with the fellowship match in hem/onc.

There were over 200 applicants granted interviews for 4 positions at the University of Tennessee. My application was stronger than before, I had clinical research experience under my belt. The result of the fellowship match was released on the same day as our residency graduation. I was awarded "Resident of the Year" and I matched into the University of Tennessee hem/onc fellowship program.

This was a double, in fact triple victory as my 3rd child, Danny was born just before I graduated residency. Working through my initial rejection with dignity and self-reflection eventually paid off.

Face to Face with Discrimination

Finally, July 2011 came and it was time to start my fellowship in hem/onc in Memphis Tennessee. Starting fellowship, I decided that I would keep a low profile so that when I would leave to go visit my family in North Carolina, no one would notice my absence.

One fateful day, I had signed up to take after-hours telephone calls for the cancer institute, fellows at the time took on this role to make a little extra money. One of the incoming calls was a gruff male voice. As I tried to find out what his concerns were and how I could be of help to him, he blurted out, "When did foreigners who do not know how to speak English start taking call for the cancer institute?"

I thought I misheard him. I asked again, more slowly this time, how I could help him, and the guy went off on me. He said "*Well, I am a cancer patient and I am uncomfortable, and I don't have the time to strain my ears or try to understand what you are saying and I doubt*

If he could hate on someone whom he did not know this much, how much hate could this guy be capable of if vexed?

that you can understand me too!". I was mortified! How can someone be so rude? I tried to maintain my composure and explained to him that I was on call but will try to have someone else reach out to him to help him. But that was not the end of this man's hatred.

About a week later, my program director called me to his office and showed me a letter that this hater had written and addressed it to the CEO of the hospital system. The letter was about 3 pages long. He told the CEO in plain language that he did not see why an

immigrant who could barely speak English would be given the opportunity to study and become a hematologist/medical oncologist.

I was surprised by the extent of hate that must have been in this man's existence. To be verbally abusive is one thing but, to take cruelty to another level with the intent to destroy someone's future was unfathomable to me. If he could hate on someone whom he did not know this much, how much hate could this guy be capable of if vexed?

Luckily, my program director dealt with this very decisively and re-assured me that the program was going to be strict about ensuring that their trainees are not exposed to such blatant acts of discrimination. His hateful actions took me down memory lane. I felt my hard work over the years was being ridiculed and scoffed at. As though I was an opportunist who somehow found herself in the hem/onc fellowship program at the University of Tennessee.

Thinking about it, I knew that I was a child of privilege. I went to the best schools in Nigeria. My parents went the extra mile because they firmly believed that a great education was the best gift any parent could give their child. I was considered smart enough to skip 2 grades in grade school. I graduated high school with honors and gained admission into one of the top 3 medical schools in Nigeria where I graduated the 2nd best student in a class of over 200 students.

I had the best performance in core medical specialties and remained on the dean's list throughout med school. As if that was not enough, I had completed residency with flying colors (with 3 babies under the age of 3 years not long after moving 6000 miles from home) and here I was, being told to my face that I did not measure up, that I was not good enough...

I could have taken this experience negatively, but I chose to make something out of it. I saw it as an opportunity for people with the same mindset like my xenophobic guy to learn a thing or two. What if I did so well during my training that I opened the doors for other immigrants like myself. I wondered.

Excelling in hem/onc fellowship took a lot of hard work and commitment but I enjoyed learning everything about it. Before the end of my first year in fellowship, my research work in thoracic oncology was accepted for oral presentation at American Society of Clinical Oncology (ASCO) annual meeting, the largest oncology professionals' meeting in the world. The research also fetched me an ASCO merit award.

In addition, I was invited to be on the team to write a protocol for a head and neck cancer grant that was submitted to the National Comprehensive Cancer Net-

work (NCCN). I was a huge success! In quick succession, I won a grant from the university to perform a translational research in bladder cancer.

Most of all, I graduated fellowship in the top 1% in the United States, that meant that if the United States graduated 700 oncology fellows in 2014, I was one of the top 7 scholars - Remarkable, Incredible, Awesome, Amazing, Noteworthy, are a few words to describe what an accomplishment it was. This was my *"Yes, I can"* moment, a moment that I have relished over and over again.

My emigration to the United States has afforded me incredible personal and professional growth. I have since graduated fellowship and currently living life to the fullest, doing what I love. More aptly put, "living the American dream". I have chosen to hold on to the beautiful memories that I created over time and to dump the bad memories into the sea of nothingness.

Life is full of choices. I am very careful to make choices that are centered around my happiness and the happiness of those who mean the world to me.

What one lesson has life taught me that I would like to share to inspire the next generation?
I have learnt that everyone experiences failure but the ability to get up, dust yourself and forge on, is the key difference between mediocrity and greatness.

What is my favorite food from my home country? Why?
My favorite Nigerian delicacy is *moimoi*. I love *moimoi* because it is delicious and healthy.

If I could thank one person in my life (living or dead) who would it be and why? I would thank my parents who inspired me from a very young age that I could be whatever I determined in my heart to be.

What legacy would you like to leave behind?
I would like to leave a legacy of love, peace, magnanimity, and hard work.

Short Bio
Obiageli U Ogbata, MD, FACP is a board certified Hematologist and Medical Oncologist, whose clinical and research interests are in Head & Neck and Thoracic malignancies. She enjoys traveling and spending her spare time with her 3 children. Dr. Oby Ogbata is passionate about providing excellent, cutting edge patient care as she hopes to close the healthcare delivery disparity one patient at a time.

Olga Calof, M.D.
Endocrinologist

The Aroma of Life

Olga Calof

UKR / WORLD

I was jolted out of my dream!

When I finally opened my eyes, I was by my grandmother's side in the teeth chattering cold of the train station depot. I was sweating underneath two winter coats and a hat. I looked around and I saw my parents, my brother, his wife and my grandmother were all dressed in similar fashion.

We were in an overcrowded hall with chipping lead paint and stale air. Our suitcases lay open with their contents on one long table. Chuckles came from the sour-faced examiners who were looking for contraband. Instead they found layers of toothbrushes sharing space with pillows, blankets, and cans of condensed milk. The toothbrushes had to be counted, and thanks to the Russian laws, required several re-counts. I could see my brother's critical gaze at my mother, and sweat starting to glisten on my father's brow.

My mother had cleverly acquired those toothbrushes to make us a lot of money. These were colorful, imported toothbrushes, with plastic cases and natural bristles. I thought it would be nice to have one to brush my own teeth with, because I couldn't recall the last time I had used one.

I tried to imagine what the heroines of the many fairy tales I loved reading would do in a case like this. I searched for an exit, but as I turned, my grandmother caught the hood of my jacket and rushed me to the train. My parents rushed with suitcases partially closed as the train was gearing up to pull out. In an unceremonious, and unprincess-like manner, I was pushed through the train window.

We found space in the caboose with two seats facing each other that could be laid flat. Like in the movie *Charlie and the Chocolate Factory*, there was just

enough space for all six of us to lay sideways. If one had to turn, everyone else had to turn with them.

Several members of our family snored.

Even though I shared a room with my grandmother and was accustomed to her melodious snoring, I could not sleep. Tears welled up in my eyes as I realized I never said goodbye to my few trusted friends. While official Soviet propaganda preached equality, non-ethnic Russians suffered. My carefree childhood was interspersed with episodes of name calling, notes of hate speech passing around during class, and an occasional chase by a local boy gang who would hide in the shadows as I walked home from school. I ran for my life, hearing curses, and dodging stones. I will fly up the four stories to our apartment, barely able to breathe. My grandmother assumed the role of my protector for the rest of my life in Kiev, Ukraine.

Our first stop was Vienna, on a Sunday, when all shops are closed. A kind neighbor donated a few bread rolls. My sister-in-law insisted on opening the condensed milk cans. The males vehemently objected. I chimed in as I, too, was famished and would have loved the sweet rich taste to quench the loud rumbling in my stomach. Finally, my brother opened one. As we looked on, he drained the contents into the sink, and took out what looked like beads. He washed them out, and showed us... Coral beads! My dad and brother smuggled them in the condensed milk cans. Still starving, I tried them on.

Our journey took us on more train rides, cramped hotel rooms in Italy, an airplane ride to New York and ultimately, Los Angeles.

In the United States, we were greeted by a family who themselves had no means to support us. To make ends meet, we searched local trash bins and salvaged a surprising amount of furniture and other household necessities that my dad fixed up the best he could.

The small amount of funds my parents were allowed, was augmented by a few liras made from the sale of toothbrushes and smuggled corals at Italian markets. My parents saved every penny, but food was still a necessity.

In my birthplace, Kiev, Ukraine, food was scarce. There were often long lines on the streets for whatever item became available and they quickly sold out. The first time my mother and grandmother entered a local American supermarket they practically fainted. They were looking at more food than they had ever seen in their lifetime. They had survived famine, war, and lifelong food scarcity, and did not understand how to deal with the overabundance of food in the United States of America.

In our former life, we had delicacies and treats only at major family events. These treats could only be available through the black market with a huge markup. In our new life, daily feasts and especially large dinners on Fridays, became the norm. Our house perpetually smelled like a bouquet of old world and novel foods my mother was cooking up when she wasn't working or at school.

The delicate peaches, pears, and ambrosial strawberries were intoxicating after drinking compote, a drink made of dry fruit, my whole life. My mother lived with the idea that tomorrow, all the food would disappear from store shelves, so we had to stock up and consume it all now!

Our neighbor had a younger granddaughter about my age. We quickly became friends. She introduced me to hamburgers. That sumptuous salty, fatty, pattie with relish and ketchup on a bun was a joy to my taste buds. One day, my new friend gave me a book, *Black Beauty*. I didn't understand a word. In my frustration, I took an English-Russian dictionary and started translating it word by word. In school, I picked up more English language skills and became more fluent.

With my new command of English, I often translated for my family whenever they needed to deal with serious issues of work, negotiation, health, and documents that I could not begin to comprehend at age ten. One day, we were visited by the FBI. The daily fear of the government coming to get us that was just starting to dissipate, returned in full force. I was worried for my parents. I felt we were watched for many months afterward.

I was kept at home, never allowed out of sight of my grandmother. This was a new world, and not safe. I was lonely in the cocoon of my family and school. My parents worked, and after work they went to school. My dreams were filled with sitcoms and books. My birthdays were largely overlooked. It wasn't until we started celebrating my kids birthdays and life events, that I realized what had been missing from my life.

I did well in school, and even got into a middle school for high achievers. "Why do you need to go so far away?" my parents wondered. My response would not have been straightforward: I recall times I was left

outside with no bus in sight, to walk home, around age 11 to 13. Sometimes, I would call on a payphone and if my dad was home, he would pick me up. I'd be scared, shivering, but kept a brave face and thought I was as invincible as Wonder Woman. There was a school much closer, but I was a teen, in my rebellious phase. I ended up having to take three different city buses. With transfers and erratic schedules, the ride took an hour and a half in each direction. Looking back now, I don't know how I did not just give up. It

My dreams were filled with sitcoms and books. My birthdays were largely overlooked.

was an escape from my home cocoon, to venture out and feel some form of independence.

After 13 years in the country, my grandmother suffered a stroke. She needed surgery, and I spent many days in her antiseptic scented room. I helped translate the doctors', nurses, and neurosurgeon's communications. I was in my senior year of college and unsure of what to do next. Get married? Have children? Get a full time job? That was the norm and what my parents were suggesting.

My parents had not gone to school here, and I didn't have many mentors. I was grateful to be in a country that had the ability to provide life-saving surgery that my grandmother would have never received in Kiev. As grandma was recuperating, I decided I wanted to help others the way the surgeon and hospital were able to help my grandmother.

I applied to medical school.

I then realized that when my parents emigrated, they were in survival mode and didn't have much time for parental guidance. In medical school, I was far away from my family, in my own survival mode. I made friends, found my strengths and weaknesses, and traveled around the country and the world. I became the first doctor in my family. While my parents helped my brother raise his kids, by the time I had kids of my own, my parents were older and needed care themselves.

One day, at work, I found a lump in my neck. It's nothing, I said to myself. I have to go to work, take care of the kids, and my parents. It grew. I developed a fever, headache, and finally not able to sleep or eat, I went to the ER and was admitted. I had a disseminated infection, which required surgery and a long post-op recovery. I could not talk for many months after surgery. I did my best to pick up the pieces. I

relearned how to use my voice. I felt like I was relearning everything, including how to be me again.

When I was little, I dreamed of being rescued by a prince. I realized that I needed to take care of myself. So, I started eating plant based foods. This was a huge change from the fast food and rich Russian food I had grown up with. This was also a big slap in the face for my mother, an amazing cook, for whom food was love. My mother and grandmother did not understand.

My immigration gave me the freedom to choose my own path. Finding my own way based on hard work and merit was a novelty. I fought the constraints of fear and glass ceilings. Most importantly, I tried to ignore the critics in my life and in my own head. I had to overcome old world beliefs about gender roles.

The loss of my mother three years ago ignited a spirit to keep our family close together. That had always been her wish. I have learned to cook Russian foods with a healthy spin. I am finding ways to reconcile my cultures, Soviet/Russian/Ukrainian/Jewish/American and keep their legacies alive for my kids.

I am committed to having gatherings of family and friends with home cooked foods and bringing back some of the fragrant dishes that evoke memories of my childhood. During such gatherings, we reminisce about the past and tell many tales and jokes. I am working on keeping the spirit of the older generations alive for my kids.

I know that this is only the beginning.

What two quotes inspire you?

"You can't connect the dots looking forward; you can only connect them looking backwards. So you have to trust that the dots will somehow connect in your future." – Steve Jobs

"Two roads diverged in a wood…I took the one less traveled by, and that has made all the difference." – Robert Frost

What one thing would you never leave home without?

I would never leave my home without kissing my kids and husband goodbye.

What one lesson has life taught you that you would like to share to inspire the next generation?

Every day presents a challenge. Trust that you can accomplish anything if you work hard.

If you could have lunch with one woman, who would it be and why?

I want to meet my great-grandmother. I want to ask her how she single-handedly kept three generations of women alive and safe during times of war and persecution.

What is your personal or professional motto?

Don't be afraid to ask hard questions.

Short Bio

Dr. Calof is a board certified Endocrinologist living in Los Angeles. She enjoys forming relationships with her patients and colleagues through teaching, writing and speaking. She loves traveling, hiking, cooking and celebrating life's events with her family; her husband, three kids and two dogs.

Finding My Way Home

Pallavi Gowda

IND / USA

This is Me

This is the rocky, bumpy journey of a lost little girl from a rural village in Karnataka, India, who later became a physician, a United States Army officer and most importantly found herself along the way.

Early Days

I often felt lost in my early days. Deep-rooted insecurities from those days still plague me. My mother died 48 hours after giving birth to me in a quest to have a boy-child. Her father, my grandfather, who was a politically powerful man was devastated by the loss of his favorite child. As a result, my birth was deemed a curse and he wanted nothing to do with me.

Realizing that her three nieces would be motherless, my mother's younger sister married my father against her own father's wishes. Seeking new opportunities, my parents left for the United States months later, with one child. My eldest sister stayed in my maternal home with my grandfather. I, on the other hand, was left in a government hospital for one year, then moved to my father's village for the next four years.

At the age of five, I was relocated to my grandfather's home and united with my eldest sister. Then at age six, I moved to America where I felt like a stranger in my own home. I spoke a village dialect of my mother-tongue, Kannada and did not know English, how to dress, or any manners or mannerisms.

I adored this "new man" who was my father. He was tall, fair skinned, and gentle. My stepmother/aunt was different. She worked during the night and was a nursing student during the day. It was evident that she had a lot on her plate and also resented my existence due to the loss of her sister. In addition to balancing a relationship with my stepmom, I was introduced to a new girl, my middle sister.

From Dreams to Reality

Despite my internal dilemmas, my family faced first-generation immigrant struggles such as discrimination with basic needs like; employment opportunities, housing placement, transportation issues, cultural differences, and overall prejudice. Before I arrived in the U.S, I pictured a place so wealthy that roads would be paved with gold.

But when I arrived, I observed a different scenery and scenario. My parents were isolated and alienated from anything similar to India. As the years passed, my family moved up to a low to middle income bracket. We were fortunate to have food, clothing, and shelter.

Uncharted Waters

Although I hail from a family of farmers who had no formal education, except for my father and grandfather, the importance of education was ingrained in me by them. Both father figures set high expectations and pushed me to surpass them in order to achieve success. On many occasions, my father's very high expectations were almost impossible to meet. We lived

in a small town, surrounded by cornfields, with very few people of color, let alone Indians. I remember feeling like Tarzan trying to integrate into society during those first few days of school in the US.

Imagine a girl walking into the boy's bathroom and hearing screaming. I did not know or understand the gendered images of the boy or girl on the door. Having no concept of money, I recall once finding a dollar bill on my desk and cutting out the image of George Wash-

Plagued with loneliness despite having people around me, I often felt I had no one to turn to.

ington, out of curiosity. I was afraid to go home that day as discipline often entailed physical pain.

Plagued with loneliness despite having people around me, I often felt I had no one to turn to. My sisters were always busy playing with each other. They did not want to be bothered with me and neither did my stepmother, who I thought hated me. I often wondered why I could not fit in. Many times, I would lock the door, lay on the floor, and just sob, often questioning why I was so unlovable.

Inner Struggles

Despite not having answers each time I would get back up and go through the motions of life. Through the years, I endured many emotional ups and downs in an attempt to validate myself to my father. I never felt good enough in his eyes and as a result, in mine. These inner roadblocks led to major self-esteem issues that I needed to overcome. This was further complicated by colorism as I was a darker, duskier, complexion than other Indians around me.

A pivotal moment in my stepmom and my relationship occurred when she admitted and apologized for not being kind over the years. This validated my feelings of pain and therefore allowed me to heal. The memories of physical and emotional pain I had endured, seemed to ease as I realized that she had emotions just like me and our relationship improved after that. Next, I channeled my complexion demons, and emotionally turbulent moments into running. Sports became my saving grace. Sports was my opportunity to express myself completely and shine while doing it. A game of tennis seemed to present a more level playing field for me, than life did.

My Army Life

I always had a strong desire to go to medical school

but was unable due to my family's limited financial resources. So, I joined the U.S. Army as a commissioned officer. The Health Professional Scholarship Program with the US Army offered a great opportunity for me to serve the country that my family and I called home, in addition to easing some of the financial burdens tied to education.

I recall wearing my Army Combat Uniform with mixed emotions as I walked up and down the halls of Walter Reed Army Medical Center. I felt pride for representing my country, but also fear since I had never met another Indian female officer. Initially I felt isolated and different, but this was not a foreign emotion. Embracing the culture of the nation's military and the camaraderie I felt, helped me confront my fears.

The Nuptial

After witnessing unhealthy marriages around me, I had dreams and aspirations of how my marriage should be. I married someone who was smart and jovial but that lasted 13 years. After going through our professional hurdles and bearing two children, his love for me dissipated and we filed for divorced. He had fallen in love with someone else, my own sister. I decided to let go after trying without success to rekindle a nonexistent flame especially, after learning that he was emotionally involved with my sibling. This caused a major divide in our immediate family with my hero, my father, supporting her. With time, I became immune to the pain and sting of their relationship. I had to deal with a new development with my father. The following months were filled with emotional separation and a deterioration of his health.

Here was a formerly well-built man who had lost so much weight that I barely recognized him. He was admitted to the hospital. I would lay next to him wondering if this was when he would finally tell me that he loved me. Instead, I found myself rubbing his feet with lotion, while his eyes communicated thankfulness even though his pride prevented him from saying any words of appreciation.

The following days would see his health deteriorate even further. He passed away 2 weeks later.

With a storm of emotions that were all too familiar, I fell into a deep depression and my self-esteem plummeted. My world became bleak after losing my marriage, my sister, and my father in one year. All those feelings of self-doubt, worthlessness and feeling unlovable rushed back. What switched me into life-living mode was the desire to see my children grow up, get married and stand on their own two feet.

Path to Recovery

With the solid support of my step-mother and older sister, I was able to get through a dark time and stand on my feet again. Today I look back and wish I could hug that little girl who did not know her worth or her inner strength. That girl who questioned if she was loveable, not realizing that self-love is the first and strongest love there is. I wish I could tell her that without self-love she cannot fulfill her duties as a mother, doctor, and community activist.

Helping others helps me feel a sense of purpose and realize that all my previous obstacles did not overpower me.

Today I feel free. Free to be me. Free to stop and smell the flowers, watch the birds soaring in synchrony in the sky or just watch my children grow. I feel free to live, love and experience all the beautiful gifts that life has to offer. To me "home" is that state of peace and self-love that allows me to view the world through an optimistic lens.

You might think my greatest accomplishment is being a doctor with a masters degree in health administration, or being a US Army veteran, or my other accomplishments. I say that my greatest achievement is self-love. That is the home we come to.

In the future, I hope to continue my community activism and support organizations that help seniors and victims of domestic abuse. Helping others helps me feel a sense of purpose and realize that all my previous obstacles did not overpower me. The future is ahead, and I plan to continue my clinical duties and expand to philanthropic initiatives that inspire me, such as improving women's healthcare and education globally.

My story demonstrates that the dream of personal self discovery is real, and achievable. Once we internalize this, we must seize all opportunities and create our own unique path. Today, I am home.

If you could have lunch with one woman (present or past), who would it be? Why? What one (burning) question would you ask her? Why?

Michelle Obama. She faced many adversities and challenges and survived them all. I am fascinated with how strong she is and how well she carries herself and inspires others.

What is your personal motto?

To love myself. When you absolutely love yourself then

you can love others and reach your highest potential. This has enhanced my friendships and relations with my children. I do not strive for the fictitious concept of perfection. The core of self-love is really self-respect; I do this by eliminating toxic self-doubt and negative self-talk.

I eliminate mental barriers that impede my ability to overcome any challenges that life throws at me. Lastly, I remember that I am not determined by my circumstances, surroundings, or the roles I serve, they only help shape the person I have become.

If you could thank one person, who would it be?
My father. He passed away in 2019 but I still liked who he was as of Friday March 19, 2019. We did not always agree on many issues due to generational differences but that made me explore ways of breaking the mold to become my own trailblazer. It is good to thank those who propelled you forward by simply criticizing you.

Mistake
My biggest mistake is not knowing what the key to a happy marriage was while I was married. I was not aware of the five love languages, how to apply them or the importance of self love in a relationship.

Now I have a good support network and I am in a place of comfort where I can reach out for work, help and empower others.

Legacy
I want my legacy to be love and honor. I think that the most valuable things about a human being are these qualities. They will weather any storm.

Short Bio
Pallavi Gowda is an Indian American medical doctor in Maryland. She is a US Army veteran, Zumba instructor, radio show host, titleholder in two beauty pageants (Miss India-DC & Association of the Kannada Kootas of America), marathon runner and proud mother of a 9 year old girl and 4 year old boy. She works with nonprofit organizations that help seniors and domestic violence victims as well as community social service activities. Learn more about Dr. Gowda at www.drpallavigowda.com

Life is an Adventure

Pat Backley

GBR/NZL/FJI

From a very young age I had always wanted an adventure. To travel the world, to see different places, to learn how other people live. But as a little English girl from a rather poor family who could never afford a car, let alone a holiday, it seemed out of the question. Now, at the age of almost 70, I find myself happily living on the other side of the world.

It all started in 1976.

I was 25 years old at that time and married to my first husband. He was offered a two year contract in the Fiji Islands, as far away from England as you could possibly get. I was so excited as I stepped off the plane into the warmth of that tropical paradise. It was so utterly different from the place and people I had left behind.

In contrast to the cold and wet English weather, it seemed exactly like heaven. Standing outside the airport, despite getting bitten almost to death by mosquitoes, I could not fail to notice how attractive the locals were. Handsome men and stunning women, all with the most beautiful smiles and skin much darker than mine.

I was so happy. This was all I had dreamt of as a little girl. To live in an exotic place, with people who were so different and yet exactly the same as me.

My two years passed in a whirl.

With the help of my new friend Naomi (a beautiful Fijian lady) I enjoyed my new country. Naomi was my housekeeper, but within two days we became firm friends and the fact that she also cleaned my house was a huge bonus!

She lived with her husband and two small sons in the flat on the ground floor of my house. I spent most of my time with her and her extended family, visiting the traditional villages and learning about their culture. I tried to learn the Fijian language, but was hopeless!

Our friendship was very deep. Two women from totally different cultures, leading totally different lives, but with an absolute bond.

I loved everything about my new home and was absolutely heartbroken when the two years was over and I had to return to boring old England, leaving my beloved Fijian family and my adopted country behind.

For me, those two years changed everything.

Whilst I have always tried to enjoy and make the best of any situation, for the next 32 years I was restless. I had now experienced another kind of living, so staying in the same safe and predictable life in England was no longer quite enough for me.

I hankered for more.

My first marriage sadly ended in divorce. We had been far too young to get married. I was barely 20, naive and inexperienced, and too soft hearted to cope with his hurtful infidelities and rather violent outbursts of temper. I tried for 14 years to make it work, but in the end, for my own sanity, I had to leave. When you feel yourself getting near to the brink of utter despair, it is time to go. When I was 41 I married a man 8 years younger than myself and became a proud mother.

In 2009 I got my heart's desire. The chance to emigrate properly this time. To begin a new life. Not in my beloved Fiji, but nearly next door, in New Zealand!

My second husband had been offered a job there, so we were able to gain Permanent Residency. Our daughter Lucy was almost sixteen when we emigrated, but she adapted incredibly well. We had visited New Zealand several times and had lived there for a year when she was tiny, so the country was familiar to us.

I loved everything about the place, the rich Maori history, the weather, the beautiful beaches and of course it was nearly next door to my beloved Fiji. As a family we flourished in New Zealand for the first few years. I was back in my happy place, on the right side of the world.

Of course there were things I missed. We had no family here. They were all still in England, my mum, siblings and friends. My beloved dad had died just before we emigrated. I tried to go back and see them as often as I could back then, and of course it is an easy 24 hour flight nowadays, not the gruelling 6 week journey by ship it had once been.

It surprised me, every time I went back to England, how out of place I felt.

It didn't really feel like my country anymore. I wasn't the same person anymore. In fact, I think I had stopped being that little English girl the minute I moved to Fiji more than 32 years earlier.

Of course emigrating to a new country is not without its problems. I will probably always feel a bit like an outsider, neither one thing nor the other.

At least I have never again been called a "Whinging Pom" (a miserable, moaning English person), so obviously my attempts at assimilating have been fairly successful!

Migration by choice, as I have been lucky enough to do, is a wonderful thing. To be forced to do so must be more difficult.

I was so happy that it was only a quick 3 hour commute from Auckland, New Zealand, to my beloved Fiji. I very quickly re-established links with my Fijian family, and was delighted when my husband suggested we build a house there.

It promised to be such a glorious time and I envisioned spending my retirement flitting between the two countries, enjoying spending hot sunny days chatting in the shade with Naomi and her sisters, whilst my future grandchildren played in the pool with all their Fijian friends... Lots of little Black and White children living my dream.

Sadly dreams often get broken or even shattered. My second husband decided after 26 years of marriage that he didn't love me anymore and wanted to return to England. Apparently he had never really felt settled in New Zealand. Although it came as an awful shock, I should have been more aware of the signs. He was not a social creature like I am, not a people person at all, and he always rather resented me being so effusive. He often told me that I *"warbled too much."*

He had cheated on me before, but then decided he wanted to stay and I just wanted to keep my little family together. So we papered over the cracks and continued. After overcoming such blips after 9 years of marriage, then again after another 10 years, I was still not prepared for it all to fall apart just before our 26th anniversary. It was a difficult time.

Especially as my Lucy was currently living and working in London. She had gone there to do her masters degree and had decided to stay for a few years. She too loved New Zealand and intended to return permanently one day, but at that time she just wanted to explore the world.

So I had to make a decision.

I was 67 years old. I was going to lose both my family home and the Fiji house, as well as my husband and the life we had planned. But New Zealand was now my home and I had no intention of leaving it to return to England.

It's been two years since that awful time and I am now divorced and happily settled into a little house of my own. I am surrounded by all my favourite things and I am content. I have created a beautiful garden and made new friends.

My beloved daughter has returned to live in New Zealand permanently and until COVID hit, I was able to fly across the Pacific at regular intervals; to spend time with my Fijian family. To watch all the babies

I am surrounded by all my favourite things and I am content.

grow, to see the teenagers flourish. To witness the two young boys, Jo and Ma, who with their mother Naomi, had shared my home in 1976 and had now become big, handsome men with families of their own.

I feel that I have two adopted countries, although technically I live in New Zealand.

Whilst they are obviously both very different from England and different from each other, in many ways they are the same. Wherever they live in the world, most people just want to have happy lives, work hard to support their families and see their children thrive.

There are of course some differences.

When Naomi died, just a few weeks before my husband abandoned me, I witnessed a Fijian funeral first hand. I was dreading it. She had been my friend for 42 years and I was bereft.

I had arrived in Fiji on a Sunday afternoon and was planning to visit her the next day.

As always, I was looking forward to a joyful day with my dearest friend. A day of hugs, stories and laughter. But I got a phone call early the next morning to say that my beloved Naomi had passed away. Her heart had just given out, far too soon. We had only just celebrated her 75th birthday.

I discovered on the day of her funeral, that the Fijian way of dealing with death is so much healthier than the restrained, stiff upper lip manner I had grown up with. In England we sat upright, in rows, dabbing delicately at the odd tear, trying not to show ourselves up by breaking down.

In Fiji that day, it seemed natural to fling myself across her coffin when it was brought to the house, stroking her face through the glass panel, weeping loudly, as many of the other mourners were doing. Not caring what people thought, I continued weeping and wailing by her graveside later that day. Such open, exposed grief was not something I had ever encountered before, but it felt so right.

My life has been so much richer because I am an immigrant. Whilst it has not always been easy, I have never regretted leaving England for a different life. It has made me a better person, more understanding, empathetic and adventurous. Less willing to just sit back and wait for life to happen.

I am very fortunate that I have been blessed with a fairly sunny nature and a strong faith in God. My life so far has proved to be so much better than anything that little girl in England could have hoped for.

When I was young I wanted to be a nurse, a missionary, an architect, an archaeologist or a writer. The 1960's were a different time. For an ordinary girl like me those were not really viable options.

But I am delighted to report that in this new life, at the age of 69, I am now a published author and intend to continue writing until the day I die. Without being abandoned by my husband and COVID rearing its ugly head, I doubt that would have happened.

If you could have lunch with one woman (present or past) who would it be? Why?
I would have loved to spend time with Maya Angelou, I feel we would have gotten along very well. She was such a wonderful survivor. Whatever life throws at you, just try to keep going.

What is your favorite colour?
I love the colour red.

Two quotes that inspire me
"O"Behind every strong, independent woman lies a broken little girl who had to learn how to get back up and to never depend on anyone." – Unknown

What is your favourite music?
I love all kinds of music (although Soul and Tamla Motown and anything played on the saxophone are my favourites!)

What is your favourite food from your home country?
I like most food, especially things that trigger happy memories from my childhood or travels. I also adore french fries and chocolate, but not necessarily at the same time!

Short Bio
Pat Backley is an author and mother to one beautiful daughter. Her published books include Daisy– a historical family saga, and her memoirs – From There to Here (With an Awful Lot in Between). She lives in New Zealand, but also has a spiritual home in the Fiji Islands. Discover more on her website: patbackley.com She is a #warriorwoman and a #sur-thrivor.

A Child of Destiny

Patience Bongwele Miller

COG

The Birth

The first girl of the proud Bongwele family is pregnant out of wedlock. And to make a bad situation even worse, the man who is supposed to be the father does not acknowledge the pregnancy.

Snares, insults, mockery would be her reality during the following nine months. Then, right out of the blue, her main support in this small community, her mother, suddenly falls ill. I was not to meet my grandmother. Despite all these struggles, she decides to keep the pregnancy. OK, the girl is born and is named Patience.

The patience my mother needed to survive the disappointment and disillusion. The girl, as I have been told, is born in the image of the father who denied her. The father she will never meet. She is cared for mainly by her mother's younger sister.

The Magic in my Hair

As I recall, my life began one summer day when I was seven years old. My mother decided to move to a larger city to attend nursing school. I was to live with her elder brother. That day my aunt, my mother's younger sister, braided my hair in five beautiful cornrows as she usually did. She said the hairdo was simple, but I looked the prettiest with it. She was singing to me almost nonstop in her soulful beautiful voice as she was braiding:

How beautiful you are,
This town is not ready for you,
You will do big things,
Your beauty is your heart,
Your heart is golden,
Your heart may break,
Remember you are destined for greatness ...

Later in the evening, she dressed me in my favorite green dress with ties on my shoulders, she had all my belongings in a round raffia basket, and we took a walk through the town.

In the distance we could hear the steady beats of drums; we could not help but sing along in unison. We walked past the catholic nuns' primary school that I attended, the high school, down through the quiet palm nut plantation, and finally reached my uncle's compound.

The next ten years would be filled with joy, loss, deception, shame, a suicide attempt, and rape; but those are stories for another day. The most important realization through this period was that I was gifted with great intellect and the capacity to love, despite the wrongs done to me.

At age eleven I lost my "mother", my uncle's wife, who had been my caretaker due to hemorrhage after a pregnancy loss. There were no competent medical staff to attend to her.

To this day, she comes to mind when I say the word mother. That was when I decided I would become a doctor for women. I later found myself attending an all-boys high school because it was geared toward biology and chemistry so that I could be prepared for medical school.

Young Bride?

Destiny will have it that someone in the United States was interested in me as a bride. I heard that he would come to visit me while on vacation but since I preferred spending my school vacations in the village with my grandfather, I did not get to meet him. The tranquility, the simple life, and the genuineness of the people in my village fulfilled me the most. Although I was happy to sit by a quiet stream in the middle of nowhere, I still felt my destiny was beyond.

One afternoon, while I was home alone studying, three men came to visit my uncle. After a short conversation, they left because my uncle had not returned home before nightfall. Before leaving, they delivered the earth-shattering news to me; they came to ask for my hand in marriage in the stead of their brother who lived in the United States. My thoughts were–

I am only seventeen,

I am about to graduate from high school,

I want to attend university,

I want to become a physician...

The next day, the delegation arrived again and met with my uncle. He told them, *"The girl you seek is my scientist, still young, and marriage is not appropriate at this time."* My uncle was a biologist and kept a lot of books, so I filled my loneliness with reading. Thankfully, he valued education and did not put limitations on gender.

A few months later, I honorably graduated from high school. The suitor continued to send letters and gifts. I began to feel connected with him and something in me believed he was the road to my destiny.

Challenges and responsibilities did come my way in my teen years and I had to mature fast; so, the responsibility of marriage did not scare me, besides, I had my own agenda. My uncle had traveled to the United States and we had family in Europe. From their stories, I always dreamed of studying abroad. I told myself that this marriage is my opportunity to do so. I, therefore, made my uncle promise in no uncertain terms that when I meet this suitor and I feel I can spend my life with him, he had to make the suitor promise that he will support my dream of becoming a physician before agreeing to the marriage.

The suitor came.

Enchanting.

Generous.

Considerate.

Loving.

Won everybody's hearts.

We traveled, visiting family for a month. I got in a small canoe for the first time while traveling to his

village. A small wooden canoe, a large body of water, I could not swim. I was shaking with fear which made the whole canoe unstable. He took my hand and calmed me down.

He felt like home.

He felt like a brother.

He felt like a father.

He felt like a partner.

I knew he would protect me.

Destiny Fulfilled

I would marry traditionally at 18, then travel to the United States as the fiancée of an American citizen a month before my 19th birthday. I spoke fluent French being from the Democratic Republic of Congo; my English was limited. I had some knowledge, from high school classes, and could comprehend while reading. The challenge was to understand when people spoke to me because it was all too fast.

Young bride, new country, new culture, essentially new language. They are likely thinking "poor thing, she is so young and away from her family." I felt like a third wheel prior to this journey, piggybacking on other people's families. Although it was just my husband and I in our apartment, I felt less lonely. He always put me first. I was home. I was happy.

I remember the first time we went to visit a family, my husband had mentioned that I just started school. The lady of the home asked what I was planning to study, and I gingerly answered, *"Medicine". "You want to go to medical school? People born here can barely get in; you probably should think of something else to do. Even the English alone you cannot speak well yet."* I would often receive similar reactions and commentaries.

I felt disappointed at times, but I knew their error was that they simply did not know me. They did not know what drove me. They did not know that this girl understood her destiny; this destiny was unfolding and that their words had no effect. I was not new to hard work; I knew very well that my transition would require hard work, patience, and understanding of people's biases.

Upon my arrival, my husband stopped his path to getting a doctorate degree and took a position as a high school teacher and soccer coach. This job allowed me to attend the sister college tuition-free. I arrived in the US mid-September 1993.

We were having problems translating my high school diploma and so I decided to take the General Educational Development (GED) test which would qualify me to attend college. We bought books and audio aids.

I spent the next two months studying all day, everyday. I passed the GED examination in December 1993, took the college entrance test at Incarnate Word College, and started college as a biology major Spring of 1994. School was not challenging; but it took some work to build rapport and friendship with others. I remember a classmate being offended because I told her she had gained some weight; in my culture telling someone they have gained or lost weight is normal. There is no undertone of judgment or disappointment.

I tried taking the Medical College Admission Test my second year of college to have a feel of it, and overall, performed decently, but my writing score needed improvement. Someone suggested I take a review course. I visited one of the centers; the fees were above our budget.

I then wrote a letter to the director of one center, explaining my situation and left it with the receptionist. In the letter I told him that I had half of the tuition and I could complete the rest helping with menial jobs at the center. I said I could clean, file, or do whatever they needed.

The director called and invited me to come and talk to him; when I got to his office, he could not stop laughing for a while. After he pulled himself together,

he declared that no one had ever made such a request to him. *"Lucky for you"*, he said, *"We need someone to put book packages together for students and tend the front office for a few hours a day."* That's how I landed my first paid job and attended the review course free of charge. Yes, nothing was going to get in my way!

By fall of 1998, I started medical school – I had a master's degree in biology, a two-year-old, and was still happily married. I managed through medical school with my husband's support, a daughter who

...I told him that I had half of the tuition and I could complete the rest helping with menial jobs at the center.

faithfully slept by 8:00 PM nightly, and a great friendship with my big sister from Sierra Leone. My sister was also married and had two kids. We supported each other in all aspects; our motto was, 'who needs sleep'? I had a sister for the first time and that felt good, no, GREAT! We thrived.

My mother came to help during my last year of medical school. She helped me nurse my kids impeccably; this brought us healing. My family had to move three times for me to pursue my dream of becoming a physician. The day I completed my residency in Obstetrics and Gynecology, I had three daughters, my always supportive husband, and my mother by my side - looking proudly at me.

In The Present

Trauma and hardships can either paralyze us and make us lose faith or make us realize that the scars they leave make our skin stronger. I CHOSE to be stronger. This was my Amen. Now I run my own successful private medical practice. I find purpose in parenting my three beautiful daughters and in helping them realize their dreams. My husband and I are now working on projects that will lead us to retirement.

What is your personal or professional motto?

My motto is accountability – I go through life mindful of my responsibilities in every situation and assume them fully.

What one lesson has life taught you?

To remain hopeful, a better day is always coming!

What legacy would you like to leave behind?

I choose to love and forgive.

If you could have lunch with one woman (present or past), who would it be? Why?

I really would love to meet my deceased maternal grand-mother. Not really to ask her a question but for the little girl in me to hug her.

What is your favorite food from your home country?

A dish called "Liwa" – made with cassava leaves, corn, palm nut sauce, eaten with yam or yucca roots. No salt or meat used.

How do you stay mentally stable when challenges come up in your life?

I have an innate state of calmness. I have learned to lead with purpose and clear expectations.

Short Bio

Patience Bongwele Miller, is a board certified Obstetrician and Gynecologist and an Entrepreneur. She is a wife and proud mother of three girls. She enjoys dancing and dabbling in singing and poetry. She is a #warriorwoman and a #sur-thrivor.

My Commitment to a World of Equality

Priti Golechha

GLOBAL CITIZEN

My mom was confused and crying. People gathered in the house were offering their condolences. My grandmother had just called to inform my dad that she had canceled her visit, as it was not worth her time. I see myself lying there next to my mom, bundled up in an old saree.

What's going on? I don't understand! Why is everyone sad? I wanted to tell them, *"Hey, I am alive, look! The baby is OK."* I finally understand that it was the unwanted occasion of having a fourth daughter instead of the long-awaited son in an Indian family. Now I was sad and baby-me was crying, and my mom was too scared to even hold me.

My dad walks in and picks the baby-me up despite the frowns from the elderly. I smell the *Jalebis* he just distributed to celebrate my birth. Perhaps, he was celebrating the opportunity he was given to build his squad of educated, independent women to make the world a better place. I see his face all brightened up and proud. I give him my first smile.

Born as a fourth daughter has been both a curse and a blessing in disguise. It was clear that if I did not advocate for myself from very early in my childhood, no one would.

When I was five years old, my grandmother finally came to visit us, to see me for the very first time. My parents sat down to prepare us for the visit. I didn't understand much of it, but all I remembered hearing them say was, "You be you! Remember, no one can take that away from you!"

While my grandmother visited, I was constantly chided and reminded of how I was "dead weight" on my parents and how I needed to be a "good" girl to fit the societal mold. One day she told me the meaning of my name. It meant *"satisfied or done with,"* symbolizing *"no more girls"*.

That was when the seeds of independence were planted. From then on, I decided to fight against anything unfair and just be unapologetically myself. But how could I do this when my name itself reminded me of patriarchal oppression every time it was called?

So, at the age of 6, I decided it was time to reinvent myself, beginning with my name. I knew I needed to do it, but I didn't know how. The subsequent worrying and stress made me so sick that I was eventually taken to see my pediatrician who accidentally called me Priti.

I was fascinated by how nicely she treated me, she made me feel empowered. Eureka! I was going to change the beginning of my story, and by that, I was going to define my future myself. I would be "Priti", a pediatrician who changes the lives of other girls like me.

I decided to retrace Gandhi's path of *"Satyagraha"*, a truth-focused, nonviolent protest. I did not cry; I simply refused to speak until my name was officially changed to Priti—meaning love.

And then, a fierce Priti was born to stump out patriarchy and oppression, not from a place of hatred, but from a place of love, overwhelming self-love.

The name change was just the beginning! Very

early in my childhood, it became crystal clear to me that the patriarchal society thrives on the oppression of the weak, and my fight was against oppression.

For instance, it was considered the norm for girls to receive smaller portion sizes of delicacies like desserts, or anything of pleasure, compared to boys. Boys were appreciated for their contribution to intellectual discussions at the dinner table, girls were required to listen quietly and clean up afterward.

> *We were treated as second-class physicians because we were "immigrants".*

Boys had the right to the bigger playground and girls were supposed to be more interested in cheerleading. Boys could wear whatever the f*** they want to wear and girls are put in a box while society decides what they wear, even as the girls are still judged for anything they choose to wear.

As I grew older, societal pressure and inequality only got worse. I kept finding myself fighting for equal portion sizes, equal rights on the playground, freedom to choose what I wanted to wear or what I say.

In order to be heard, I knew I had to be a "some-

body" first. With sheer determination and an eye on my goal, I knew that one sure way to get there would be through academics because that had never been hard for me. So, without much effort, I got accepted into one of the best medical schools in India.

Medical school was, however, a huge culture shock and possibly the lowest point in my life. At home, I knew my fights and I was enough for who I was and loved by my parents. In medical school, for the first time in my life, I was all alone, away from home. I was not prepared for the blatant ostracism I experienced. I was "invisible" because I didn't speak English or wear fancy clothes.

Unseen and intimidated, I began to shrink inside myself, rarely speaking up. So, slowly but surely, I started giving back exactly what I was receiving - Hate! I wanted to be successful at any cost. I wanted to show them I could be a "good" girl who fits right into societal expectations.

I decided that becoming a gynecologist was a perfect path to achieve success for me, another woman. I worked like a machine with no emotions and no joy. I had let the oppression win and now I was feeding into the system. Deep down, I was dead, I had given up, my grandmother had won, patriarchy had won, oppression had won.

One morning, I could not take it anymore, the pressure, the hypocrisy almost paralyzed me, I could barely move in my bed. I left everything, quit medical school and returned home.

I was again surrounded by the loved ones who believed in me, that slowly brought me back to life. I reconnected with my school friends. That was when

---

We were treated as second-class physicians because we were "immigrants".

I noticed this guy, Gaurav, who was always there for me, cheering me on. He supported me and my fights against inequality, from the playground to the larger issues. He was not overwhelming in his masculinity despite my stance against patriarchy. We fell in love instantly and decided to get married.

Before I got married however, I wanted to be independent. So I decided to pursue my lifelong dream of becoming a pediatrician. If that was not possible in India, then so be it. I would spread my wings and fly!

I decided to come to the USA, I was fascinated by the history of this "free" country. I secured a pediatrics residency in New York. Only then did I discover

that this country, built by immigrants wasn't built for immigrants, I faced oppression again because I didn't fit the master narrative, because of my skin color, my immigration status, my accent, how my food smelled...

We were treated as second-class physicians because we were "immigrants". The others made sure we knew our place. Some of us spoke up against it, but our concerns were never validated. Though I had it bad, my Black and Hispanic sisters had it even worse.

I wanted to do something. I could not go back to the place of darkness that I had worked so hard to escape. But emotionally, I wasn't yet at a place to speak up. I needed to heal first. This time around, I didn't run. I finished my residency.

I got a job in a non-profit community organization in a small town in California, where I could work for the underserved, the migrant workers, and the underprivileged, the presumed underdogs like me. Working as a pediatrician, I started advocating for my patients and their families, making a difference. It was the best thing that could happen to me professionally. But, something was still missing, I found myself struggling with repressed memories of oppression.

I avoided those feelings as I was finally living my dream as a pediatrician. I was giving back. I got married to my proud feminist high school sweetheart, my Gaurav. The days were bright and went really fast. Before I knew it, I was pregnant with my first child, a girl! And I could not be happier.

But on the day of the first ultrasound, it hit me!

How could I bring her to this unjust, unfair, patriarchal, misogynistic world?

> *"The fierce "Priti" needs to take action now!" I told myself.*

I was comfortable in my bubble, but patriarchy and oppression were alive and kicking right outside, waiting for her! And the day she was born, I swore that I would do everything in my power to move that needle.

"The fierce "Priti" needs to take action now!" I told myself.

I started seeing things differently at work. In healthcare, women are given second-class status from the top-down because the business of healthcare leadership lacks equity. I decided to get out of my comfort zone and fight back.

This was going to be my legacy, for her and for every other girl to come!

I applied for a Regional Medical Director posi-tion that was way out of my league of qualifications. I worked hard to build alliances, create influence to make sure I get the job. I did get the job and numerous promotions! Yet, I felt it was still not enough. I needed to empower other women, pull them up, to make a greater impact.

I created a judgment-free platform for women physicians to connect, seek advice, mentor and coach each other with a mission to get more women in leadership. I founded an organization called Physician Women in Leadership. Thousands of women all across the USA started reaching out. Today I mentor and coach women physicians to help them find their voice, to advocate for themselves. Most importantly, I empower these women behind the scenes!

Today, I have two daughters who mean everything to me, I have a tribe of thousands of kickass physician women in my community and more importantly generations of girls who are watching me.

My ultimate goal is to leave a legacy for them, where they can proudly say that I used my voice to create a world of equality where every girl deserves respect and dignity. I want every little girl in this world to know that she is capable of everything and anything despite her gender, color, or immigration status.

I am committed to creating a world where every girl knows she is enough.

Personal Motto

Align with your values, strive for excellence, you will be loved for it and you will be hated for it, but do it anyway. Do it for you!

Who to thank

My daughters - Chloe, and Keisha, for making me who I was supposed to be all along, the fierce "Priti".

Favorite food

Dal Dhokli, my traditional comfort Marwari food. Every time we eat this meal as a family, I feel I am surrounded by love and nostalgia. I am continuing a yummy tradition that I am proud of.

Lunch with one woman

Brene Brown. Her coaching of being vulnerable instead of striving for perfection strongly resonates with me.

How do you stay mentally stable when challenges come up in your life?

By self-reflection and asking the right questions. I take some quiet time reflecting, documenting gratitude for good moments, grace for bad ones and creating a safe learning space for myself. Instead of asking "Why do I feel this way?" "Why does this keep happening to me?" I ask open-ended questions "What is going on?" "What were my triggers?" "What can I learn from this to help me move from victimhood to a growth mindset?

Short Bio

Priti Golechha is a first-generation immigrant, a physician executive, a national award winner, a mom of 2 girls, and a lifelong learner. At her day job, she serves as Associate Chief Medical Officer for a nonprofit community organization, Golden Valley Health Center in Central California. After Medical school in India, she did her pediatrics residency at Mount Sinai Medical School and Elmhurst Hospital in New York. She identifies as a fierce feminist.

She is the founder of the "Physician Women in Leadership" Organization and in her spare time, she blogs about her experience as a BIPOC Healthcare Executive. She mentors and coaches early and mid-career women physicians to help them climb the leadership ladder and empower them with authentic leadership skills. Priti can be contacted at https:// pritigolechhamd.com

...For a Better Future

Sharon Shiraga

TWN / USA

I was 10 years old crying in an all-girl dormitory in Taiwan. I was the youngest and smallest amongst the students in the class. I missed my sister and parents terribly, and wrote journals and letters home daily.

Time and time again, I would ask myself the same question, *"Why am I here all by myself?"* The answer was always the same, *"This is an excellent school and you would have a better future".* My family had always planned for the future, and this mentality initiated a cascade of long journeys away from home.

1989 – the news about Tiananmen square student protests broke internationally. China-Taiwan relations were unstable. My grandparents were part of the Chinese Nationalist Army that retreated from China just before the change of regime.

As immigrants to Taiwan, my parents were terri-fied of being caught in the conflict between the strait. For better education and the future, my younger sister and I were sent to the United States when I was only 12 with high hopes and dreams. In principle, it was a great idea with an ultimately good outcome, since I now have a beautiful family with a great career. However, the journey was countered with too many hurdles and too many tears.

My parents had to stay in Taiwan to make a living for my expenses while I lived with an aunt during our transition to the US. I knew my aunt from Taiwan and remembered her as being quite strict, but she was always nice to me back home and when I first arrived.

For reasons unbeknownst to the teenage me, my aunt and my parents had a falling out and she ended up taking it all out on my sister and I. While I was learning a new language and trying to fit in at school, there was constant verbal and physical abuse at home. We had to cover up bruises and cuts, when we didn't know how to process things, she would scold us - *"Your parents were no good, thus you are no good"*.

I was physically and emotionally torn apart with the constant verbal degradation, unexplained disciplinary action, and incessant threats of deportation. It was a time before the internet, I was able to connect with my parents once or twice a month via brief landline calls. The calls were expensive and my parents were trying to save money for our college tuitions.

As good Asian daughters, we didn't say much about the abuse and perhaps I didn't understand the gravity of the abuse. It wasn't until I learned about psychiatry in medical school, that I realized I had been a victim of domestic childhood abuse and neglect growing up.

Looking back with a clinician's eye, my aunt herself was likely suffering with depression as an immigrant. As psychiatric conditions are often unrecognized and a taboo topic in Asian communities, she needed help herself and we were the unfortunate victims of her suffering.

At the same time, I was also the surrogate parent for my younger sister. My parents had asked me to care for my sister who was 4 years younger. On one hand, being the older sister kept me responsible. On

the other hand, despite my best effort, I failed as a good parent at age 12 which is not surprising to the adult me. However, that sense of inadequacy lingered for decades.

Through the turbulence of my teenage immigration journey, the only stable thing in my life was schooling. I had control over my studies and my knowledge which I excelled in. Staying focused on education connected me with lifelong friendships and helped me make better choices for myself.

I must have been a toddler when my grandmother played word and number games with me. With her

Through the turbulence of my teenage immigration journey, the only stable thing in my life was schooling.

patience and encouragement, I sorted out the puzzles and found the answers that were always there. She told me stories about her childhood as the only daughter of a wealthy merchant in China. Her family owned a huge house the size of a large city block, with many servants. Her fortune was lost in the Chinese Civil War through her own immigration journey.

Girls had not been allowed in schools, but her father was a generous donor. He had taught her puzzles and games when she was a child. He wished for a better future for her. My grandma knew that she had to do better than the boys in class and strived to be the top of her class. She told me "never give up on your dreams and believe in yourself". These words echoed in my heart and kept me focused throughout the years.

I received my first C grade in history class during my first year in the US. I was old enough to know that this was not a reflection of my intelligence, but I was frustrated with the language barrier. I remember looking up every single word in the history book about the US civil war using a paper English-Chinese dictionary.

Despite memorizing the textbook, I still had trouble answering the questions because I didn't understand the vocabulary in the question. Being a straight A student in my pre-immigrant life, a C grade was difficult for the young me to accept. I held on to my grandmother's words and believed in myself to work even harder, and it paid off. I started English as a second language (ESL) as a 7th grader and finished with honors English by high school graduation.

High school was a strange time. My clothing was different from the rest of the students. I didn't have the cool hair of the 90s nor the baggy pants with over-sized plaid shirts. I wore foreign appearing clothes with tights, thick glasses and puffy hair. People may or may not have laughed at me, I wouldn't know due to the language barrier.

My insecurities made me question everything people were saying around me. They may or may not have been talking about me, but I couldn't tell. I was in a dark place both from the negativity around me, and from the fears I created myself. Then, life threw a golden ladder at me in the form of a best friend in high school.

We both sat at the corner of the history class together and although she had her own struggles, she saw that I was in need of help. Our love for Manga and video games created a bond that led us to endless conversations.

She was the sunlight in my darkest stormy days.

After I left my aunt's house at the age of 18, my best friend's family accepted me as their own and I had a place to go for holidays and birthdays. She was the family I always wished I had, and the family I chose.

While obtaining a minor in Mathematics in college, I was approached about being a doctorate candidate in math, which I declined. I didn't think I would fit in with the group. I didn't see anyone from my background – a shy Chinese immigrant girl. So, after college, I was lost.

I worked multiple jobs for a while; a barista, secretary, medical biller and research assistant. Through the basic science research and great mentors in life, I was exposed to medicine and decided that this was somewhere I could do some good for people.

Moving forward to medical school, one day, during my obstetrics rotation, my chief resident remarked with all seriousness in her voice, *"you are going to be*

"Me? A surgeon?" I thought to myself. I didn't have the look of a surgeon. I didn't have the confidence of a surgeon.

---

a surgeon". I laughed. *"Me? A surgeon?"* I thought to myself. I didn't have the look of a surgeon. I didn't have the confidence of a surgeon. I wouldn't fit in with the group. The excuses were endless.

However, I excelled in technical skills. I enjoyed the complexity of procedures and the knowledge that came with understanding the anatomy and the pathophysiology of diseases. My love for problem solving was on overdrive in the operating room. I finally found my niche.

Surgical residency was one of the toughest training programs as we often worked over a hundred hours a week. While on the transplant rotation, we once received 12 donor kidneys within 3 days. Despite working restlessly with progressing hand cramps, all twelve patients got their organs and produced urine for the first time in years. There was finally a sense of accomplishment that brought satisfaction to my work and meaning of success.

The girl who was too shy to join the math club was now the only female surgeon in a conference room...leading projects.

The rigors of residency gave me thick skin to be confident for my patients and to be a strong minority immigrant leader. It was an evolution! A victory over my inner revolution. The girl crying in the dorm room was no longer crying. The insecure girl who didn't know what she wanted now had goals. The girl who was too shy to join the math club was now the only female surgeon in a conference room...leading projects.

Now, I have two beautiful children of my own. I wish for a better future for my children without the hurdles I endured. I also wish so deeply that they would understand the path I traversed to bring them into the world.

My past defined my character and made me a fierce woman warrior for a better future.

What do you do to relax, unwind and refill your cup?
This may be unorthodox, but video gaming is my go-to for de-stressing my days. Schooling and surgical residency were highly demanding to say the least. With the luxury of little free time, I connected with friends and family via gaming.

We played online competitive first person shooting games, multiplayer battle arenas and situational survival scenarios. It was a mode of socialization with a purpose through teamwork and quick decision making processes.

Gaming has given me the skills to be a strong leader in collaborative group settings. One would say that I gained hand-eye coordination skills that translated into surgery.

What one thing are you most proud of as an immigrant?
Early on in my immigration journey, I wanted to fit in with my peers so much that I was determined to speak with an American accent. I asked my best friend to correct every enunciation and avoided words until

I got the tones exactly right. It took years! Nowadays, it would be difficult to tell my accent unless I am sleep-deprived after a long surgical hospital call shift.

What is your favorite food from your home country?
This food can not only be described by the taste, but also by the smell - the stinky tofu. The dish gets its distinct smell from the fermentation process.

It is comparable to the smell of boys' old gym socks, with a texture of old sponge, and yet, amazingly delicious. For expats from Taiwan, this food brings back the nostalgia of bundling up with the family, and enjoying street foods with small folding chairs and dim-lit streets on the sides of a busy market.

What one lesson has life taught you that you would like to share to inspire the next generation?
Through my immigration journey, I learned that I am a fighter and a survivor. One may say that a person is shaped by the obstacles they encounter along their way. I often wonder if I had stayed in my home country, would I have been a successful physician today?

I also wonder what would have happened if I didn't have my immigration journey? Perhaps I might have grown complacent and not aimed higher than I thought I could.

Life is not only what we've seen in the past, but what we envision going forward.

In what ways do you think migration has made you a stronger person?
I often refer to the first six years of my immigration journey as the darkest period in my life, they are the skeletons in my closet that I want to bury forever. However, knowing that I not only survived neglect and abuse, but also became a beacon for others, it gives me the confidence to not be fearful of any hurdles in life.

Short Bio
Dr. Sharon Shiraga is a board-certified General Surgeon who practices in Sacramento, California. She specializes in stomach pathologies from laparoscopic procedures for gastric cancers to treatment for benign reflux. One of the rewarding aspects of her job is being an educator of residents and medical students as a guide for the future of medicine. She lives with her husband and two beautiful sons.

She enjoys traveling, the outdoors, and time together with family. She plans to take her children to Taiwan often, to allow them the opportunity to experience her culture first hand.

In Loving Humanity…

Shwanda Ifeoma Onwuachi

NGA / JAM / USA

Growing up in the American diaspora, I sometimes chuckle at the conversations that frequently got me the weird stares among classmates in my high school cafeteria, they often happened as we discussed the food we ate or things we did over the weekend.

We would discuss what we would do with the monies we earned from our part-time-after-school gigs. Rightly so, I would speak of what I knew, what was familiar to me, thinking that even though there was a difference, surely teens are open-minded enough to embrace those differences, right? Teens are supposed to be the most open-minded subgroup there is, right?

I savored the thought of pigging out on chicken feet, rice and peas, and stewed plantains. I would share my love for the foods that were common in my home with the same excitement that my classmates shared their love for pizza, burgers, or chicken strips with fries.

I recall it being the first time that I was met with opposition, and it was expressly stated, *"What kind of backward, foreign crap is that? Who eats chicken feet?"* I laughed along with the group that I called friends, even though I knew they were laughing at me and not with me. Often, the jokes at me came with the typical stereotypes towards Africans; lions, monkeys, elephants, etc.

The Good, The Bad and The Other

Going to a predominantly African American school from a bi-cultural home, initially I was not well received. I did well in school and my teachers loved me. I transferred with ninety-three being my lowest grade. I recall my English teacher, jokingly telling the boys who were smiling at me, the new girl, *"Now boys, don't get your undies all up in a jumble, she's smart and I can imagine with these grades she came with, getting her education is probably top on her list. She is not studding you all."*

My English teacher was a beautiful African American woman from New Orleans. She had fair skin with beautiful dark naturally straight hair, and I remember she smelled like Aramis. It is a perfume that most women around her age purchased from Foley's, the departmental store. I loved her accent. I often would look in the mirror and try to mimic her accent, but I could not quite get it right.

What my English teacher did not realize was that my good grades had a lot to do with my Nigerian, Igbo father. You see, any Nigerian will tell you, while things are not universal in some cultures, we have things that are common to children of Nigerian parents. So, to my father earning anything less than an "A" in school meant that somehow, I was doomed to work at Mac Donald's and was most likely not going to be the doctor, engineer or attorney that he had already told his friends I would become.

Me having good grades was a spoken expectation in our household. Nigerian parents often take their children's achievements or the lack thereof, personal. And true to culture, daddy lived vicariously through his children. We have a groupthink mentality, as it were. Everything the child does or does not do is a direct reflection on the parents: well, that's exactly how it was in our household.

I went to school with such pressure to always be above my peers, I could hear daddy saying; actually, it was a part of the lexicon in our home, *"You shall always rise above your peers in all that you do. It is in your blood, you are African. You are Igbo."* He did not realize the pressure that caused me, being a teenager, an "A" student and feeling like the whole of the Igbo culture was on my shoulders.

Not to mention, my mum on the opposite side exclaiming how much I owed to the West Indian culture and their sacrifice to come to America. She would talk about how coming to America was only to ensure that we had the best that life could offer and to them, America was the Utopia. Earning good grades and making them proud was the only reasonable show of appreciation.

My experience in secondary school led me to realize that though Black, I often was not seen as Black enough for many of my peers. I was even confronted one time by a classmate during Black History Month. She stated, *"Jamaicans aren't Black!"* This was so confusing to me because I look Black, my mum looks

Black, even though she calls us West Indian. We are still Black, nonetheless. I began to question my identity, until I concluded later in life that *"It doesn't matter what people call me, but what I believe about myself and respond to."*

Fitting in was quite difficult for me even though I am a very friendly person. I was not quite Nigerian enough for Nigerians; not Yardie enough for Jamaicans because of my Nigerian mixture, and not "Black" enough to Black Americans. Being a chameleon became commonplace. When I was around daddy's family, I would try to speak pidgin. I would speak in my Jamaican dialect around mum's people, and slang while learning the newest R&B songs around my Black American friends. It was exhausting!

My teachers became my refuge, all African American, and most, not all, willing to embrace me. My economics and government teacher was a stout African American woman, who wore her hair the same way all the time in a short bob, cut slightly high in the back, with the sides slightly longer than the back. She had a beautiful cocoa chocolate complexion, wore very little makeup, and was always dressed in the best professional designs.

She wore heels every day. Her appearance as a teacher made an impression on me and is the reason

that I am known today for my fashion sense and wearing high heels as I teach daily. She would casually tell us on Monday morning that she went to the beauty shop that weekend. I personally never saw the difference.

However, she was one of the most impactful teachers in my life. My reason for having a love for education is directly related to her, and my eleventh-grade English teacher who introduced me to the Harlem Renaissance. I was in love with education from that moment on.

Assimilate, *"the process of taking in and fully understanding information or ideas" (Webster Dictionary, 2021)*. The word assimilation partially elucidates my experience as a first-generation American born girl-child to my parents. The dichotomy of striving to be All-American as it were, staying true to my mother's West Indian, and Nigerian father's cultural pride, often left me feeling dissipated as it related to culture at all.

I lived my life attempting to please so many different sides of myself culturally

---

Maneuvering through three cultures many times became grueling, and even though I see myself as a Black woman today, I can say that I somewhat understand the opposition that many multiracial people feel. Growing up with bi-cultural parents often left me seeking acceptance in knowing that I was ok.

I lived my life attempting to please so many different sides of myself culturally, thus I found myself losing a part of who I needed to be for me, the person that I was meant to be. Unfortunately, I did not become acquainted with myself until later in life.

In doing the work on myself, I burned the bridge of feeling a certain way about Black American people, Nigerians, and West Indians. In some way I felt that each subgroup played a part in the insecurities that engulfed me for a good portion of my early life. One day, I said to myself, *"I don't care. I am going to choose a side and stick with it"*. I choose today to identify myself as Nigerian-American.

I used to feel guilty about leaving out my mum's culture. I often felt some kind of way, when I would speak partial Igbo and my mum would correct me and say, *"You're also West Indian. Don't leave me out"*. And even considering being fully aware of who I represent, I have stood firm on my declaration of being a Nigerian-American. It is just easier for me.

When it came to Black Americans, I had to come to the realization that holding animosity against a group of people that are without a doubt, the long-lost kinsmen of my ancestors made no sense. I owed it to myself and my daughter, whose father is African American to respect a people who have a strong history of overcoming great tribulations, yet thrive in a land that they have made home (by force).

To me, that is something to be celebrated and not looked down upon and abhorred because of my experience as a youth. I have come to appreciate that what

I felt was directly connected to the fact that I wanted to be a part of a culture that did not want me, and it hurt like hell.

Being married to an African American man only served to validate my experience as a youth when hard times arose. My struggle to move past hurts and disappointments that I faced in my adolescent years, among diasporans, came like a tidal wave when heated exchanges or indiscretions would take place in my marriage.

What I found so profound about me was that the same vitriol that I felt for African American women, I did not feel for African American men, until the typical friction points of any relationship surfaced. Not until recently, and through positive relationships with African Americans, have I learned that it is unreasonable to brush an entire group of people with a broad stroke. Daily I am growing, and I have been able to temper those feelings of bitterness and the superiority that daddy would often mention that we were, simply because we were African.

The Evolution

I see people as the valuable human beings they are. All of us with a story that includes tribulations, trials of life, and triumphs. When it is all said and done, we are all in this together, and that is a good thing. We are stronger as a unit than we are apart. When we see people as the valuable contributors of this great thing we call life, without the labels, we are all valuable.

What one lesson has life taught you that you would like to share to inspire the next generation?
The lesson in life that I would like to share to inspire the next generation is; learn to embrace who you are fully. Do not look outside for love, but learn to love who you are inwardly. There are so many people in this world that are trying to find their way and have not learned to be fully accepting of who they are. Unfortunately, those people can hurt you if they have not healed themselves.

Hurt people, hurt people. Once you learn to fully accept and embrace yourself, flaws and all, you will allow people to be their authentic selves. When people show us who they are authentically, and because you've fully embraced your self worth, you will not make excuses for their misbehavior or lack of authentically loving you.

Learning the skill of self-love at a young age will prevent many of the pitfalls in life that you will inevitably encounter. Self-love and acceptance includes being keenly aware and listening to your intuition.

What you are seeing or feeling is, so don't ignore your spirit. Trust yourself enough! Be enough for yourself. Care enough about yourself. Live the life that you were created to live.

What is the biggest mistake you have ever made? What were the consequences? How did you correct it?
The biggest mistake I ever made was marry a man for his looks and success. My goodness, my ex husband is so handsome! If success were a picture, it would be him. Wrong! I lived and I learned, and it was fruitful while it lasted. I changed that trajectory today and it is all about my core values.

How do you stay mentally stable when challenges come up in your life?
I have learned to center myself in the word of God. I speak positive affirmations to myself such as I am whole, I am the head and not the tail, I am blessed and can not be cursed, I am loved and accepted. I speak what I desire into existence.

What one thing would you never leave your home without? Why?
I will never leave my home without my cell phone. I am such a relational person and leaving home without my phone would mean that I am not accessible to people that I need and need me. Moreover, my phone contains so much of my life. I can't function without it.

As a child, what did you want to be when you grew up? Are you doing that now? Did emigrating change or affect that in any way?
When I was young, I wanted to become a teacher and a soldier. I am a teacher today, and I served in the United States Army. I got to live the dream that I desired. I was born in America, to a solid upper middle-class family, my home life was free from distraction.

Short Bio
Shwanda Ifeoma Onwuachi is American born to a Nigerian father, and Jamaican mother. She is the eldest of 4 children and the only girl. Affectionately, called Ada by her late father, Shwanda's passion is educating the next generation, the field in which she believes her calling has led her to for fourteen years. She is currently pursuing a doctorate of education in curriculum, instruction and assessment. She has one daughter, who is currently a college sophomore. Shwanda often says, "one of her greatest achievements in life was the Lord giving her Amaka as her gift." Shwanda can be found on social media: Instagram: @shwandaonwuachi; Facebook: @shwandaifeomaonwuachi.

Tope's Journey

Tope Fapohunda

NGA / USA

Sitting on my bunk bed while in middle school in Nigeria, I would sometimes find myself daydreaming about being in the United States, but I would quickly snap back to reality knowing that I had to pass my final exam before I could visit. My immediate family had already relocated to the US while my twin sister and I still lived in Nigeria. I loved visiting the US for shopping, constant electricity and water, and for bragging rights that would often last longer than the visit upon returning to Nigeria.

We were only supposed to come for a fall break and go back to Nigeria afterward. "It is expensive to bring you two girls to America to come visit us multiple times", my mother complained. "We are not sure when we are going to finally return to Nigeria." "You either stay in America or you can return and remain in Nigeria until we come home...We don't know when that will be..."

So my journey began...

It was not planned, nor anticipated. I was sad for the first two weeks that I'd left everything that I knew behind, my friends (without any contacts), and extended family. I didn't get a chance to say goodbye to anyone, or pack my prized possessions. So I initially mourned my things, but the tradeoff was living daily with my family, and that was worth it. It would be great, an endless vacation, or so I thought.

We started school that fall. Being a naive teenager, I didn't know how mean teenagers could be...yet. The accepted hierarchy amongst older and younger students in Nigeria did not exist here, a younger student would respect the wishes of a senior, but outside of that you weren't torn down or degraded, as was my experience here. In Nigeria, we all wore our uniforms to school so there was no disparity between you and your fellow classmates based on the way you dressed. Initially, my looks, to me, were secondary. My clothing was simply something to cover my nakedness. I thought having an accent that was different from the others was just the way things were. Alas! It wasn't...

I had always been taught that going to school was very important, education was paramount for success, and it should be taken seriously. So when I started school here I was a nerd without even knowing it! My first priority was to get good grades and get my education. But all that changed very quickly.

When you don't know what the accepted norm is, teenagers can be very cruel. They would constantly point at me as I walked the hallways, snickering and laughing sometimes covertly, but many times overtly, I was forced to take a second look at the things that I considered "secondary".

I developed a morbid fear of going to school. I was constantly ridiculed for being smart. Fifteen minutes to the end of every hour my anxiety would flare up, knowing I had to brave the hallways again. It was terrible! Once I entered the classroom I would countdown till the bell rang again. I knew once the teacher started speaking I would be safe.

Each day, I couldn't wait for the bell. I practically ran out of school, alone.

I wouldn't say we were rich in Nigeria, but there I wanted for nothing. Here in the US, I qualified for free lunch, and had a three dollar a month allowance to go clothes shopping at a thrift store. My dad ate tuna sandwiches with an apple for lunch everyday so we could save money. My mom worked in a different state and came to see us three times a year.

While I felt safe at home, we did not live in the best part of town, so hanging around the neighbor-

You are an outcast if you don't go with the masses. You are ostracized and torn apart if you don't comply.

hood was not safe and the school wasn't safe either. My school was nothing but a place of mental anguish and emotional stress riddled with self-doubt and anxiety. I questioned everything about myself. I realized I might be different from other kids, and different is not what you want to be in high school.

You are an outcast if you don't go with the masses. You are ostracized and torn apart if you don't comply. I struggled a lot because a part of me knew that THEY were wrong. I struggled with the notion that even though my skin was darker, and I talked with an

accent, wore dated clothes, and actually wanted to get A's in my classes, it did not mean that I was less than. I struggled with believing that I was worth the air I breathed, that my existence in this universe mattered.

I did not know it then, but I was bullied. I cried alone a lot. In addition, my body was changing physically, and I had nobody to talk to about it. I thank God for the stability, strength and confidence that my parents instilled in me that carried me through. I had to learn to reprogram my brain from being goal-oriented and education-centric to this stranger whose self-worth began from their external appearance.

I was mostly disappointed because I felt that the people that looked like me treated me the worst. It seemed the people who really accepted me without question were the people who did not look like me. It also seemed that the people who did not look like me were the ones who were in school for a purpose.

I remember having a 3.9 GPA at the end of the 10th grade year and making an appointment with my Black guidance counselor to enquire about Advanced Placement (AP) classes for the next school year. I wanted to be challenged in class. I still remember her words, "I don't think we should put you in any AP classes. I don't think you'll be able to handle it, let's just keep you in the courses we have you enrolled in".

I was in disbelief. I left school that day despondent and defeated. How could she hold me back when I was excelling? How could she believe that I should accept the status quo and not push myself further? I had no idea how I was going to make it through another year in that school.

Thankfully, a month afterward, we moved out of the apartments, into a house, in a new school district! This was my do over. This was my chance to put into

---

I was no longer ashamed to be African, to have an accent, being nerdy or of getting an "A".

---

practice all that I learnt about social acceptability. I was not going to let the color of my skin, or the style of my hair, or my accent prevent me from moving forward. I wasn't going to allow people's perception of me to dictate how I felt about myself, my friends, or what I could accomplish.

That fall, at the new school. I joined every club that I was interested in. The nerdy clubs like math club, and the socially acceptable clubs like drama club. I was no longer ashamed to be African, to have an accent, being nerdy or of getting an "A". That was who I was,

some people will accept and appreciate it, and some people will not. And that was OK with me.

I knew who I was, so my NEW journey began!

State two of your favorite quotes and why?
"Do unto others as you would want them to do to you."
It speaks to treating everyone, regardless of class, race, or stage in life with basic respect and decency. If we each treat people the way we would want to be treated I believe this world will be a much better place. This is more complex than it seems.

Treating people the way you would want to be treated sometimes means learning about those people. Case in point, what brings you comfort may not be what makes others comfortable.

First you need to know what makes the other person comfortable to be able to provide it. Regardless though, the goodness in your heart that makes you want to treat others as you want to be treated will prevail, and shine through.

"A flower does not think of competing with the flower next to it. It just blooms." -Zen Shin
I like this quote because you'll find that many times, part of what prevents you from really enjoying the space you're in, is the fact that you are comparing

yourself to the space that somebody else is in. Each facet of your life has its own beauty, just like a flower. It might also have thorns, but people pay attention to the beauty of the flower and not the thorns.

Similarly, most people are enjoying or seeing the beauty in you, not the thorns or imperfections. Lastly, the flower concentrates its resources and energy on making itself the best that it can be, so we should stop comparing ourselves to others or trying to attain what others have.

If we spend more time concentrating on making ourselves the best that we can be, we would enjoy life more, be happier, and become more beautiful.

How do you relax?

For me relaxation is traveling. Seeing a different part of the world, seeing and being able to appreciate a different view of the world, observing different cultures and value systems always excites me. But of course, traveling is also almost synonymous with vacationing and not working, and that's enough to unwind. If I cannot break away and travel somewhere, then retail therapy is my relaxation.

What is the biggest mistake you've made?

The biggest mistake that I have made, or that I've

continued to make, is not living in my truth. When you don't live in your truth, you live in bondage. And when you're living in bondage, you cannot reach your full potential. Living in your truth is what makes you beautiful, those imperfections that you try to hide are part of what makes you unique. Living a sham, or as others want you to, is usually living in a shell of who you really are. I have made and corrected this mistake many times, and it remains a work in progress.

What is your favorite dish?

My favorite dish from my home country is something called *efo elegusi* with goat meat. It's somewhat like a spinach stew with ground pumpkin seeds and obviously the meat is from a goat. I know it's probably an acquired taste, but I love it, and most people that have tried it, whether Nigerian or not, love it too.

Who would you like to thank, past or present and why?

I would have to thank my parents. My mother: I learned selflessness, the value of hardwork, and sacrificing for other people's good.

I learned that regardless of your age, you can always improve and evolve. She taught me not to be enslaved to anything and that anyone can survive under any circumstances.

Ironically, I also learnt that I like luxurious things and got the love of shopping from her. Luckily, I've been able to thank her but unable to thank my father. He taught me integrity, honesty, fiscal responsibility, and that vulnerability does not equate to weakness. He also taught me that free expression of love is a beautiful thing.

Short Bio

Dr Temitope Fapohunda is a board certified Obstetrician Gynecologist and Entrepreneur. She has her own practice "Every Woman's Ob Gyn" where her goal is to heal her patients physically, medically, and make an impact in their lives. Her passions include volunteering, both in the United States and through medical mission trips to Nigeria, networking with fellow Nigerian physicians to make a difference in her communities, and spending time with family. She is married to an awesome husband and has two children. In her spare time, she loves decorating, shopping and craft work.

A Journey of Faith and Hope

Yvonne Kangong

CMR / CAN

Chasing the Dream

I was born in Cameroon, West Africa and lived with my parents until the age of 3, when my parents moved to the United Kingdom (UK) to study. During those days, when I found myself alone, I would sometimes look up to the sky at the sound of a helicopter or aeroplane, yearning for when I would be reunited with my parents. Other times I would simply say to myself, "One day I will get into that and fly far away."

I spent most of my childhood moving from one relative to another in various cities until the age of about 11 when my parents returned to Cameroon, after which my brother was born. Those were the years that ignited my love for travel.

At the age of about 11, I started dreaming about becoming a doctor. I had always looked up to doctors and couldn't wait to become one. I went on to secondary school in both Yaounde and Buea, where I took my General Certificate of Education (GCE). I tried applying for medical school in Cameroon, but was unsuccessful, so I left for Nigeria where I did an undergraduate in Microbiology to get me better prepared.

Back in Cameroon, I applied for a United States visa to join the rest of my family, who had moved there when I was 20 years old but was declined (this would be the first of many). Why didn't the US grant me a visa? Why did it have to be so complicated when I already had family there? I pondered.

Life in St. Lucia

Moving to a land far away with no family members, to become a doctor? Yes, that had been my dream, and nothing would stop that. I arrived at St Lucia, and set-

179

tled down thanks to the support of my dear belated mom, my dad, and the rest of the family. School went well, and after nearly 2 years, I still didn't have my US papers.

My mind became flooded with the following questions: What is next? Where do I go from here? What is going to happen to my career? Too many questions to answer. In the meantime, I moved to Trinidad and Tobago to spend some time with my friends while I reflected on the next step.

Never to Forget

I spoke to my family most days, and this one night, I shall never forget. My mom called me on my friend's house phone. We chatted, laughed, and all was well. She told me she was going to work, so we said our goodnights and goodbyes. I went to sleep. She went to work. The next morning, I woke up to the sound of nonstop phone ringing in the house.

I just wanted to sleep in, but finally decided to get up as the phone's constant ringing was so annoying. I got up, came to the kitchen, and I could immediately sense some uneasiness around the house. I asked what was going on and was told "nothing really". I was instructed to eat as it was late. Breakfast was already waiting for me, so I ate. My friends sat me down and

told me that my mom was found on the ground at work and was now in intensive care.

How do I swallow that? Where do I begin? Should I scream? Should I cry? Should I yell? Should I be mad at why this is happening to me and my family? What happened? Was I a bad girl so this had to happen to her? Had she been working too hard to pay for my medical school? Why did I even want to become a doctor if it had pushed her to be in the hospital now?

What will happen to my dad and younger siblings who had just moved to the US?

Owning my Grief

I summoned the courage and called my dad, and from the tone of his voice I knew things did not look good. He said, *"Mummy was found on the floor by a co-worker who came to relieve her from her shift, she is in the Intensive*

I lived my life attempting to please so many different sides of myself culturally

---

Care Unit and it does not look good." "What? But I spoke to her last night and she was fine." I wailed. I prayed for God to bring her back, but God had a better plan for her, she had to go to her Creator to be one of His angels. Few weeks later the life support was discontinued. I was told that she had shed tears towards the end of her life as my dad was talking to her.

I wish I could have read her mind at that point.

My rock was gone, my strength, my everything. How do I continue medicine? I must make her and the family proud. Her funeral was to take place in Cameroon, so I decided to apply for a US visa to pay my last respects before she was taken to Cameroon

to be laid to rest, but the visa was denied yet again. So, I applied for a Canadian transit visit with the help of a family friend in Canada. I got the visa to transit through Canada to bury my mom.

I had planned to return to Trinidad. But there was really nothing waiting for me in Trinidad upon my return, so I decided to stay in Canada.

North American

I arrived in Canada in November of 1999 and wondered, *"What do I do?"* Thus began the immigration battle that lasted 6 years, and earned me the deportation list, twice.

I kept praying and fasting throughout that period and was blessed to have met a fine young gentleman, who became my husband and the father of my kids. We had to work in factories and call centres to pay bills, and sometimes even used food banks.

We are now blessed with 3 kids, maybe I should just forget about being a doctor altogether. Here come the naysayers, *"Stop wasting your time on this dream of becoming a doctor, so many people went to medical school, and they are now taxi drivers, factory workers, etc."* I almost gave in to that, but I have a very supportive spouse who encouraged me. I had my sister too, who has sadly passed away, encouraging me.

I held onto this Bible verse daily, Isaiah 40:31: *"But they that wait upon the Lord shall renew their strength; they shall mount up with wings as eagles; they shall run, and not be weary; and they shall walk, and not faint."*

On Being an Immigrant

Life is difficult being an immigrant. You must work extra hard. I am proud of the lessons that I learnt along the way. They have taught me to be resilient, to be grateful for every day, and to reach out to others in need. I do not take anything for granted. If I see someone in need, I will reach out to support them to pave the way for them as I do not want them to have the same struggles I had.

No, to the Empty Cup!

"You can't pour out of an empty cup." I have no idea who said this quote, but it is so true. When you have negative energy in you, everyone around you feels it and this affects everyone around you. So, to prevent this, you need to make sure to take time to rest, to reflect on life, and to refill your cup, to be you.

Before your career, family, etc. you were you. You spend time alone with yourself in your brain 24/7 so that the brain must be at peace. I love to eat healthy and exercise. During COVID-19, I have gotten into skipping ropes and doing about 500 per day. I pray, sing, go for walks/runs, practice yoga, meditate, and spend time with my family and friends, which keeps me going and happy.

Lesson For Generation X

Use failure as a learning opportunity. I grew up with the saying, *"If at first you don't succeed, try and try again."* We had to memorize this quote and say it daily at school. It looked like a chore then, but it has helped me throughout my life.

Gratitude

Always have an attitude of gratitude. Be grateful and say it daily, together with positive affirmations. You must be grateful. It is a privilege to be alive. Gratitude is everything and has been linked to our overall well being. When you start counting your blessings, you forget about all the challenges in life. So, focus on the things you are grateful for and see what a difference it makes in your life.

My Favorite quotes

Personally – *"Whatever comes out of your mouth, should be to raise someone"*. I love this quote because words are powerful, and it can either make someone see their

potentials or make them lose confidence in themselves. Why would someone ever want to hurt anyone with their words? I ponder. This quote started when my kids were much younger, just to remind them to watch their words. It originated from watching movies and hearing them tell their siblings 'I hate you' when they had a fight. This was a reminder to them that this was not tolerated in the house, and your sibling is your best friend.

Professionally – *"Let food be thy medicine, and medicine be thy food"* - Hippocrates

I like this quote because it reminds me to always look at non-pharmacological methods of treating medical conditions, rather than depending on medications alone. This has helped me focus more on a holistic approach in my patient population.

Have lunch with one woman?

My late mom. This would be such an amazing opportunity. I would tell her everything that has happened since she died. I will introduce the kids, sing and dance with her. I will also get into deep conversations to ask her why she died when we needed her the most? What happened exactly on the night she died. I would like to hear her experience in the intensive care unit, how did she feel when they were taking off the life support?

I would like to ask her these questions because I feel like she died prematurely, while helping the family, or was it because of helping me in medical school? I will also ask her if she is spending quality time with my late sister and the rest of the family gone before us. I will ask her to teach me songs and how to sing better.

One thing that I cannot leave my home without

Praying as a family. 1 Chronicles 16:11 says, "Pursue the Lord and His strength; seek His face always."

Biggest mistake I have ever made, consequences, and how did I correct it?

I will go back to my childhood. My dad was not yet home, and a family friend came to our house and my mom gave my dad's food to this uncle. While I was taking the food to the uncle, I stopped mid-way and asked my mom why she is giving my dad's food to this uncle and what my dad will eat when he gets home. I had to write 'I will never do that again,' 1000 times. That was the end of the story and never repeated itself!

How do I want the world to know me?

I want the world to know me as the woman who loved God and loved to smile. My faith has seen me through very difficult times, and I have learnt to always lean on the Lord. I also want the world to know that smiling is contagious. It might just be that last hope someone needs. Smile because it is good for the soul. Smiling releases endorphins (feel good hormones), which have a positive impact in your life.

Short Bio

Dr Yvonne Kangong was born in Cameroon, West Africa. She is a wife and mother of 3 children. She is also a speaker , coach, mentor, a family and obesity medicine physician, public health specialist, and clinical lecturer at the University of Calgary, Cummings School of Medicine.

She is a certified transformational coach and founder of Breaker's Health (www.breakershealth.com), a medical consultancy practice and co-owner of KFS BBQ smokehouse and market. She loves empowering people and giving back to communities. She volunteered in Haiti in 2015 for a medical mission. She loves singing, dancing and spending time with family and friends.

You can reach her on social media @ drkangong@breakershealth.com. IG; @drkangong. On LinkedIn, Clubhouse and Facebook: Dr. Yvonne Kangong

THE
WARRIOR
WOMEN
PROJECT

THE
WARRIOR
WOMEN
PROJECT

Lightning Source UK Ltd.
Milton Keynes UK
UKHW050107090621
385147UK00002B/77